Feline World: Feline Coloring Book

Explore the Beauty and Majesty of Felines in Vibrant Colors!

I thank God for everything! And I believe that God is what gives meaning to our lives, God tells us to love our neighbors. I love you all.

This work sought to show different felines for coloring, reminding us of these beings that live among us, make the most of it.

Jucinei Silva

2024

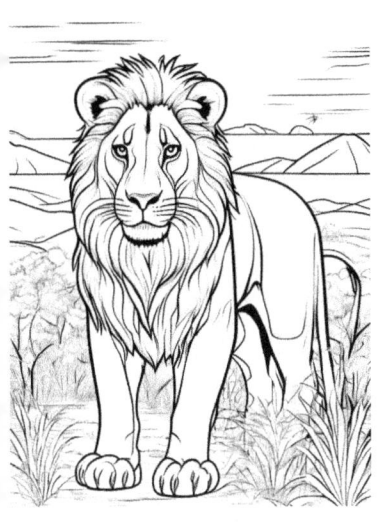
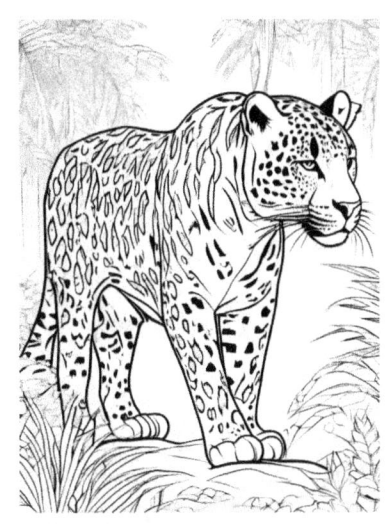

This Book Belongs to:

|_____|

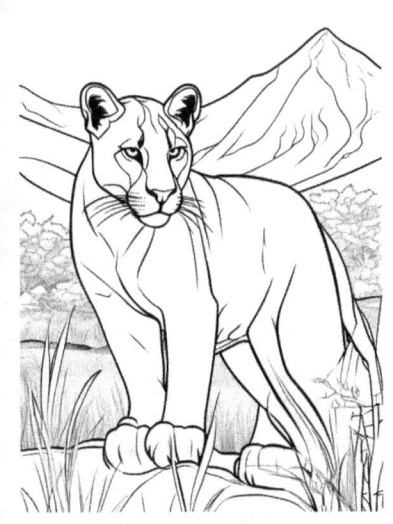
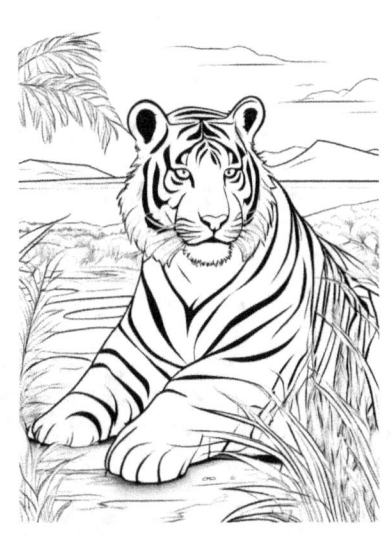

J.S.P.©
Ali rights reserved

ALL RIGHTS RESERVED ©
2024

No part of this publication may be reproduced, distributed, or transmitted in any form or by any means, including photocopying, recording, or other electronic or mechanical methods, without the prior written permission of the publisher, except for brief quotations incorporated in critical reviews and other specific noncommercial uses. Any unauthorized replica of this work is prohibited.

J.S.P.©
Jucinei Silva Publications

Test Color Page

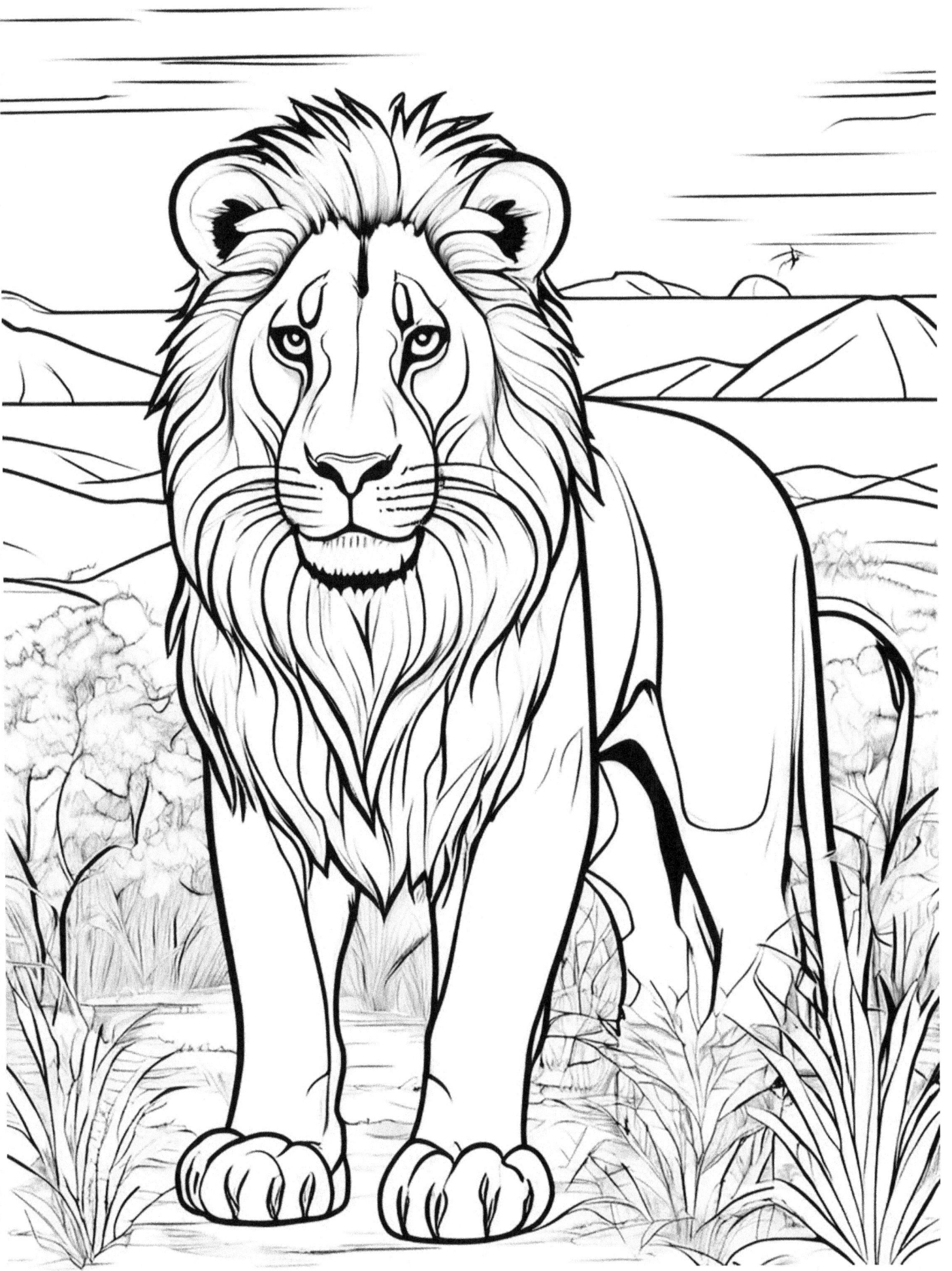

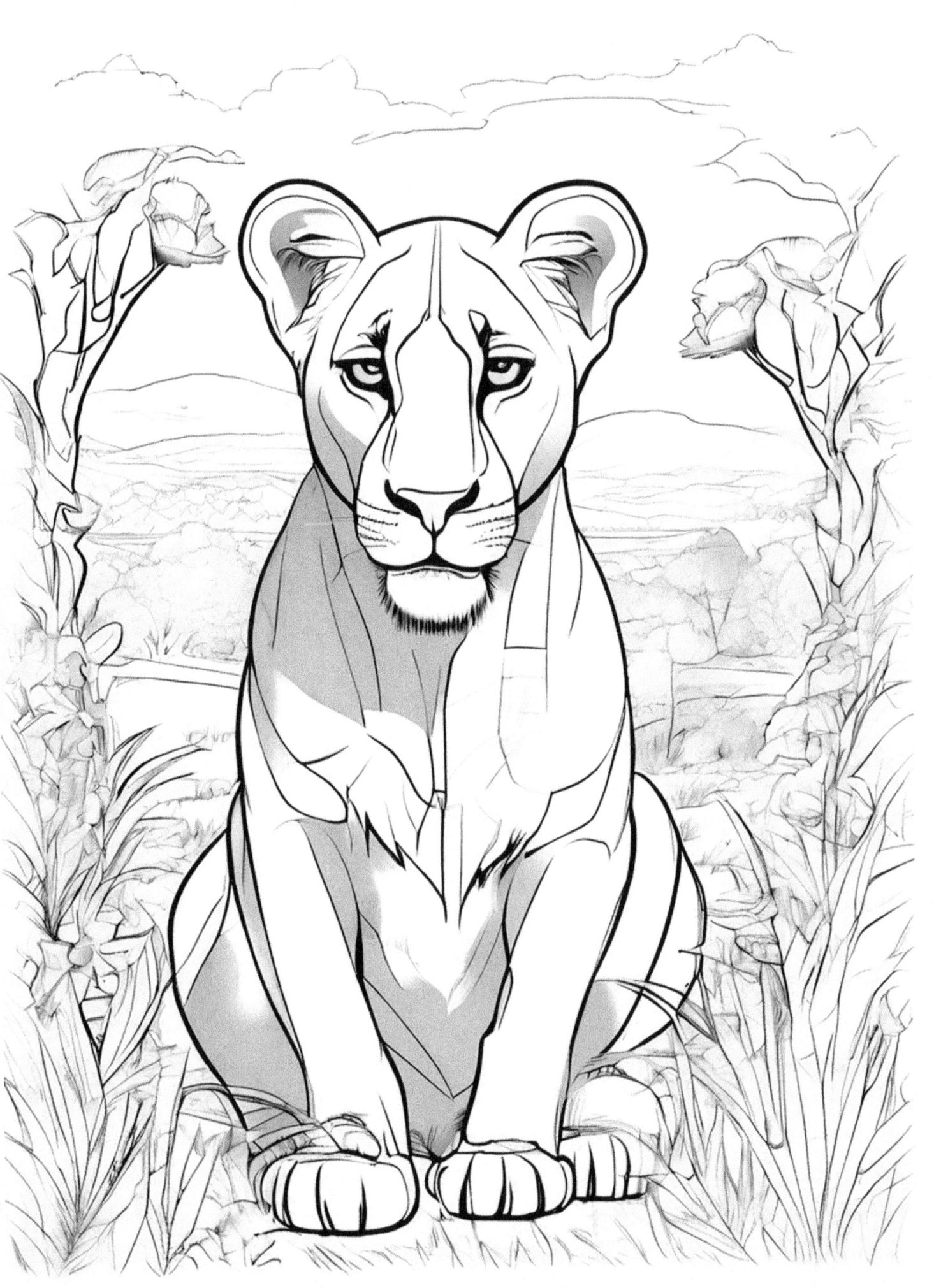

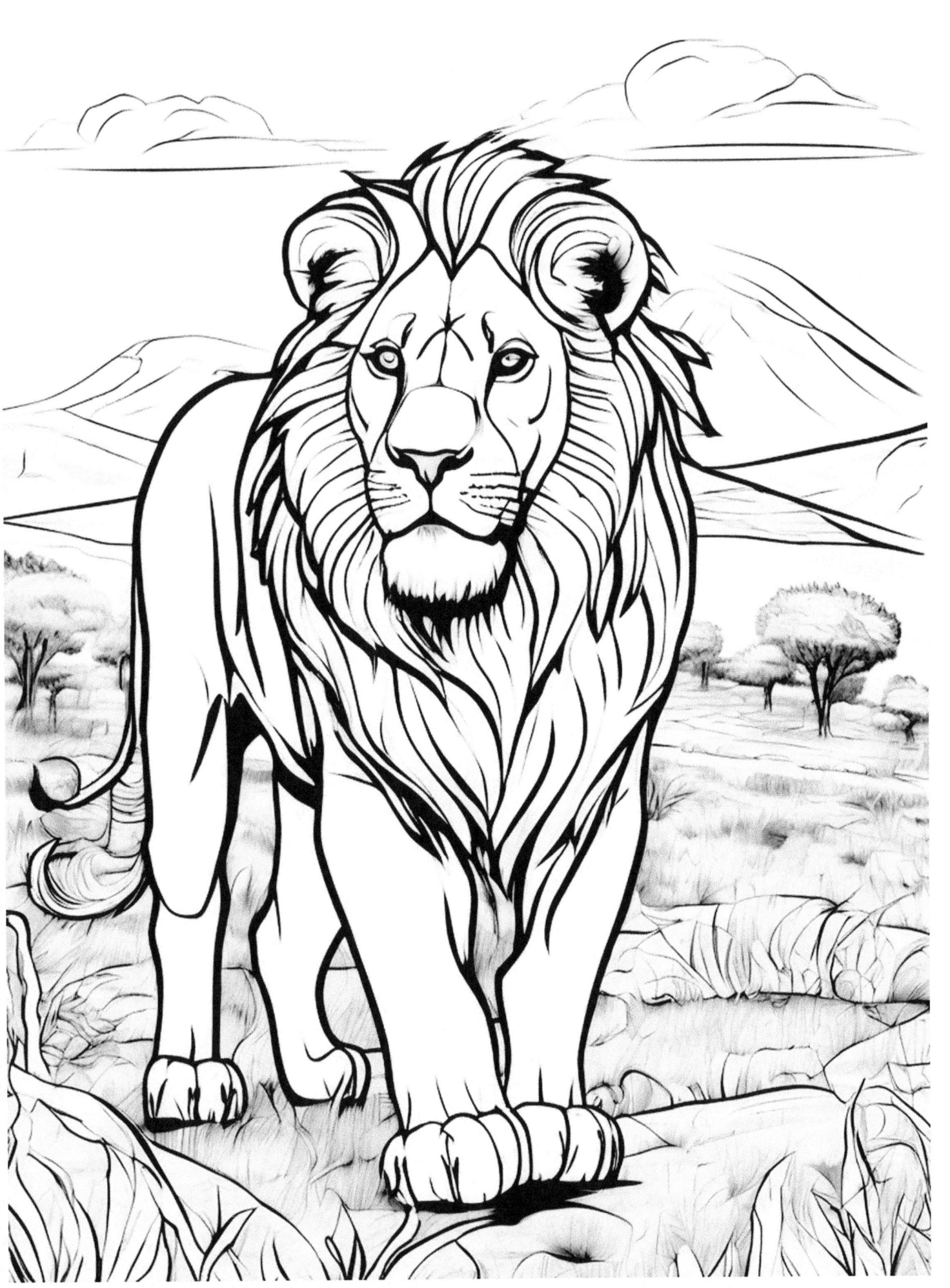

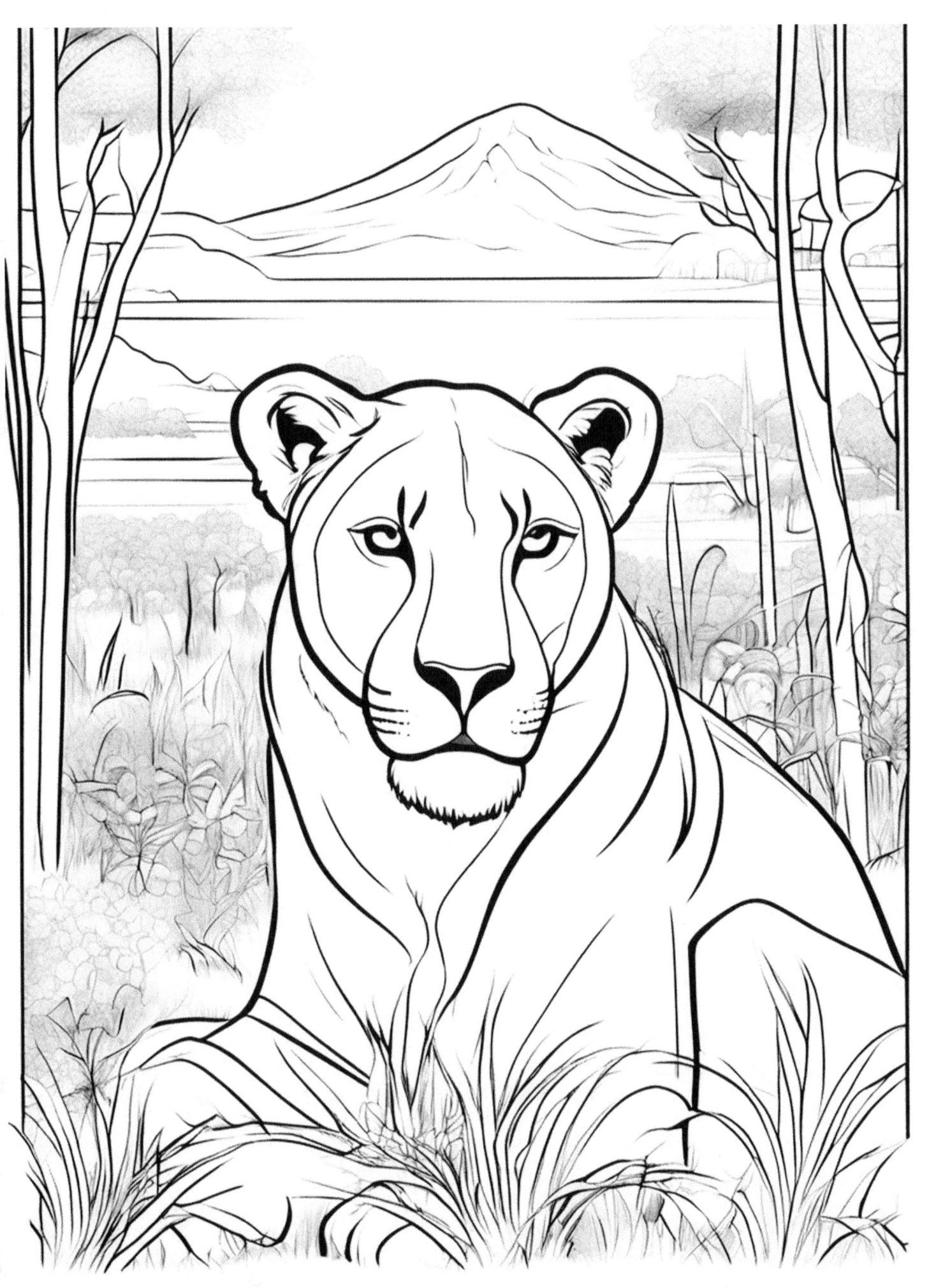

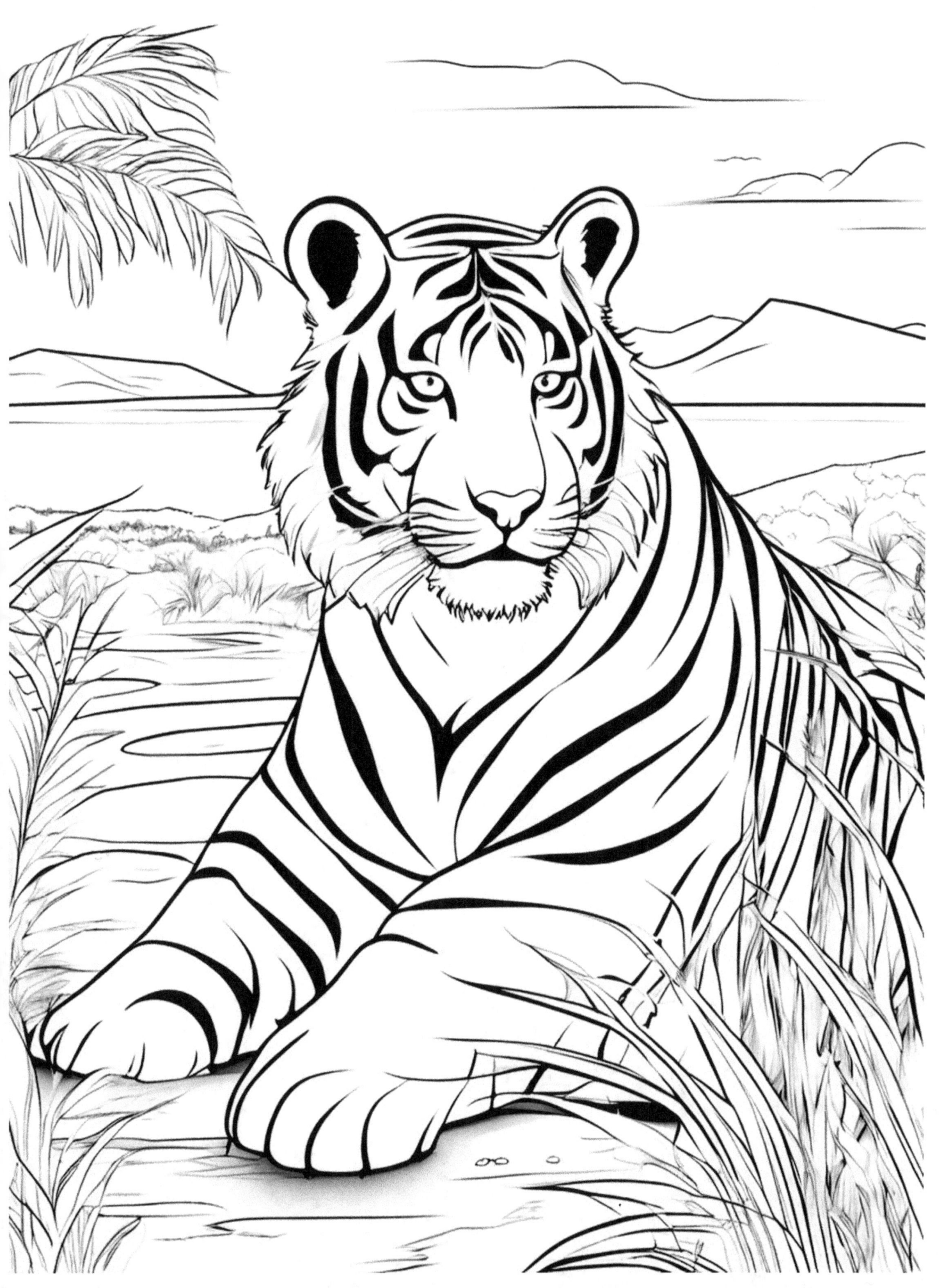

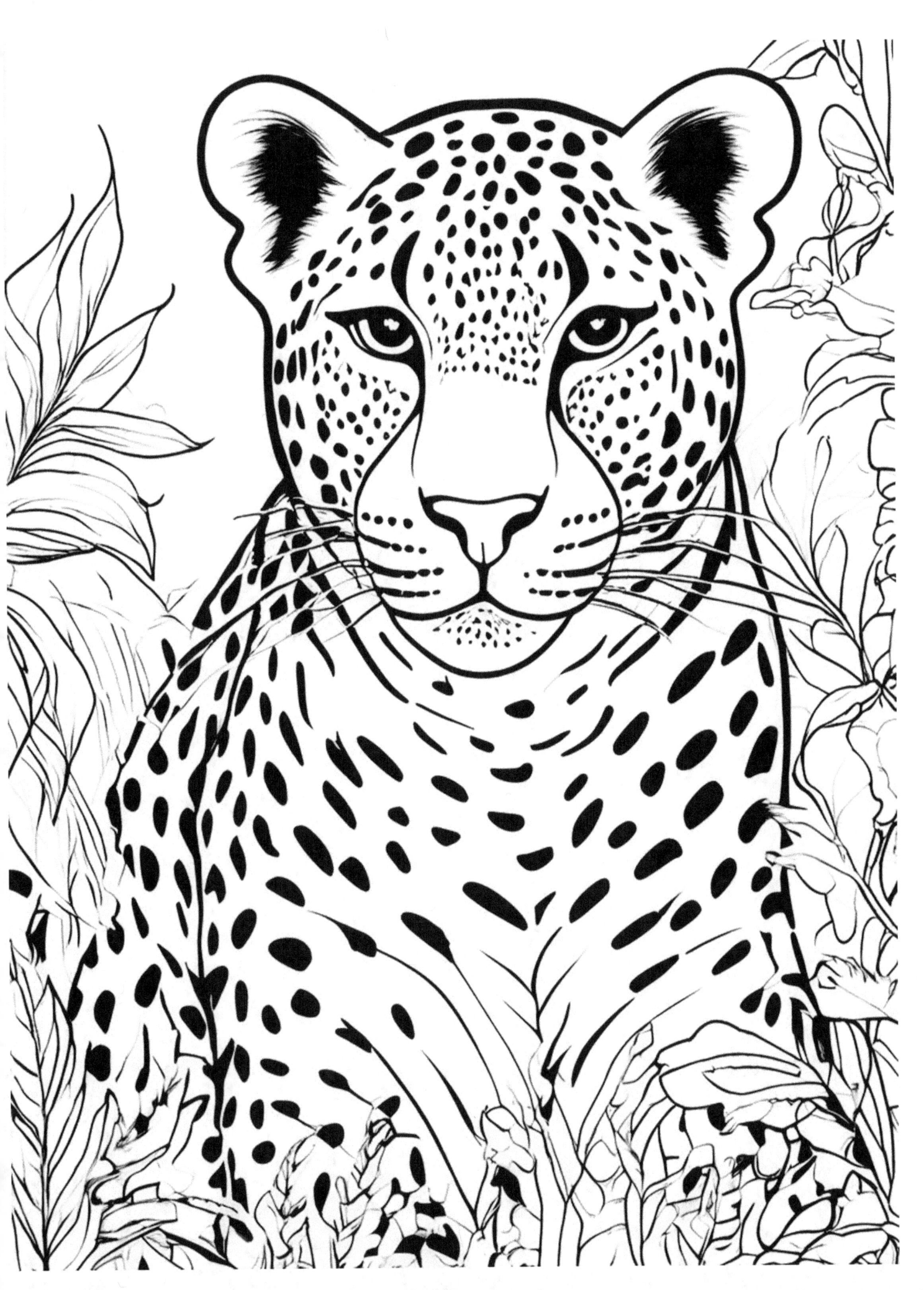

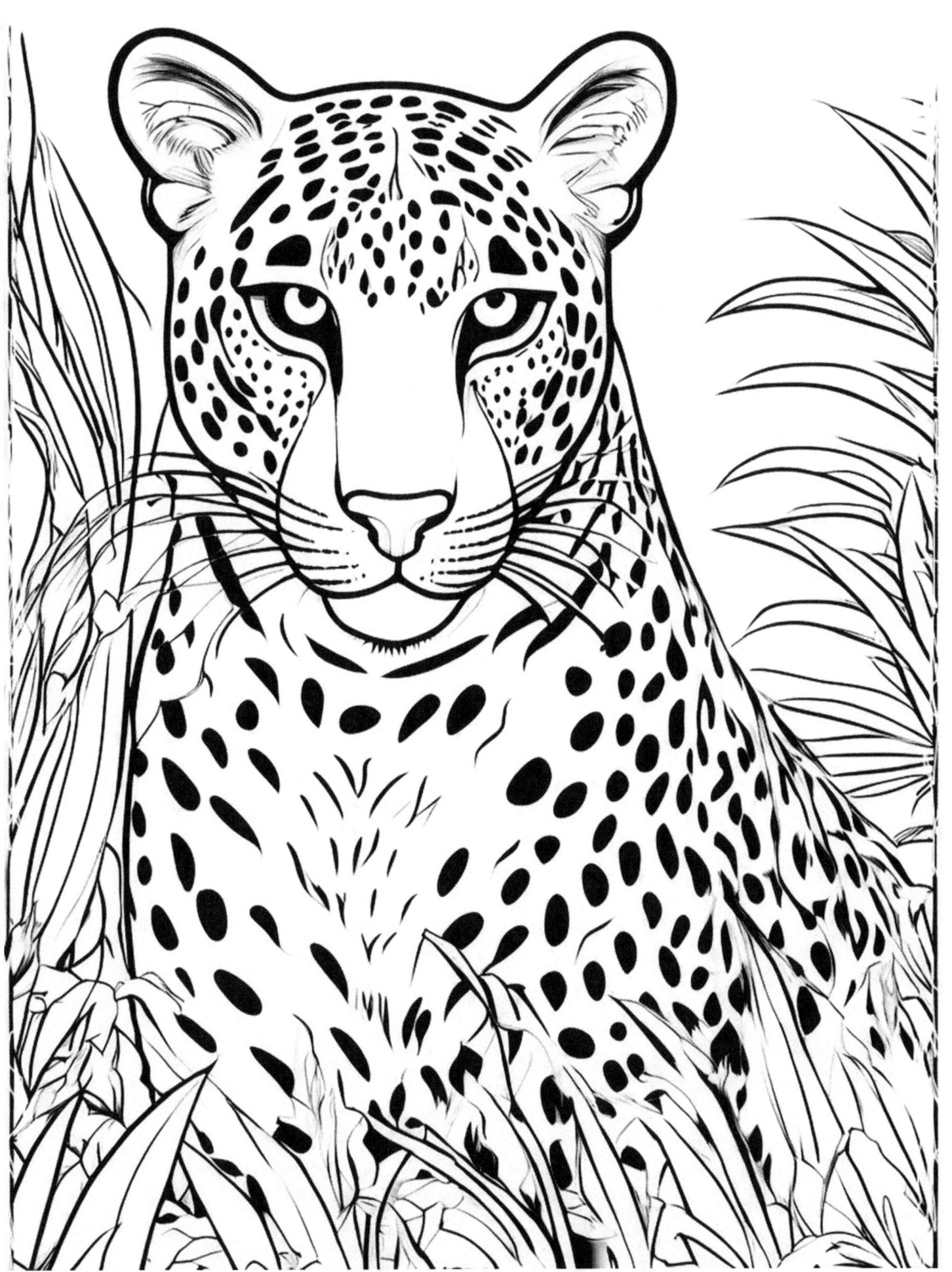

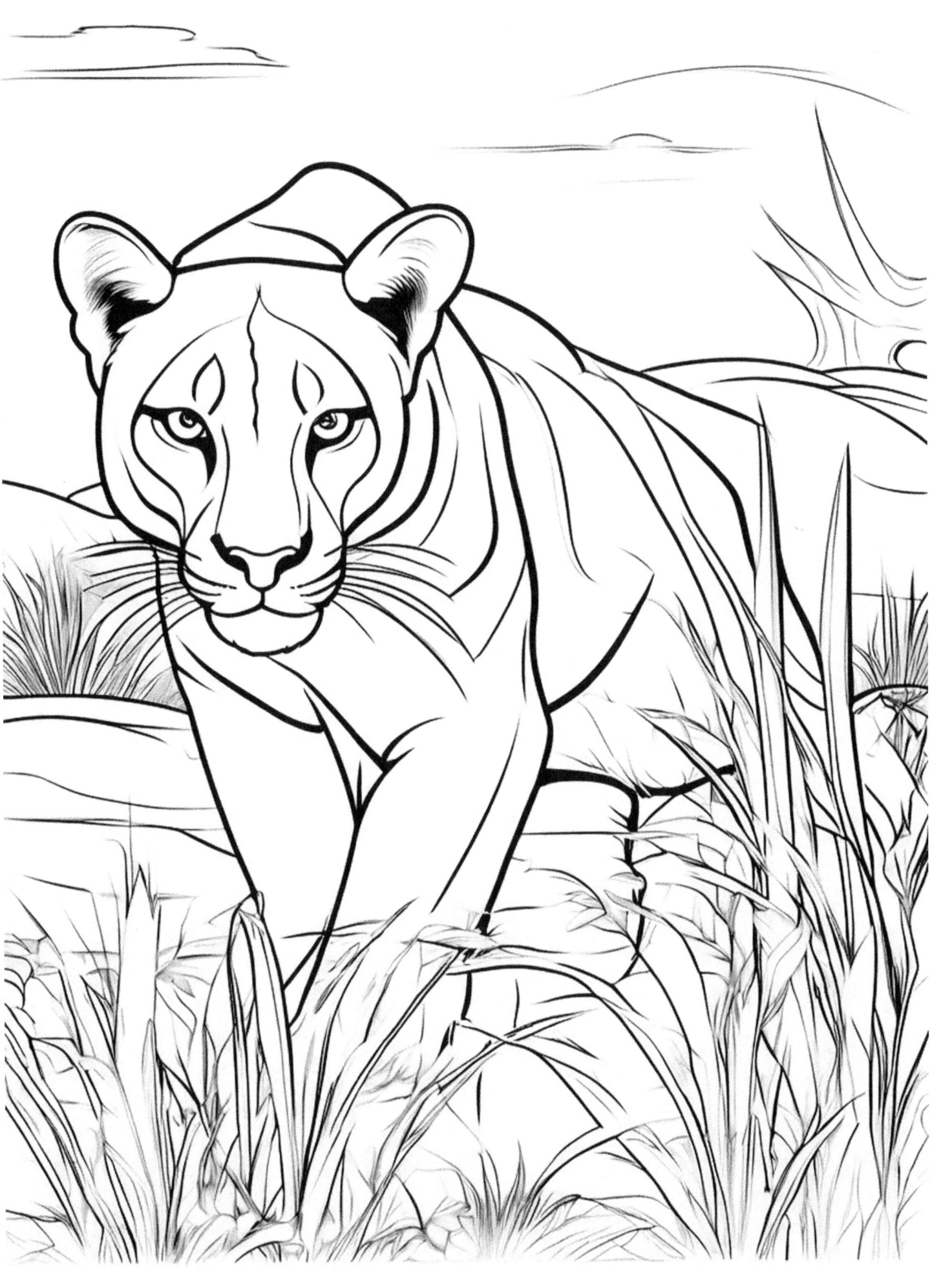

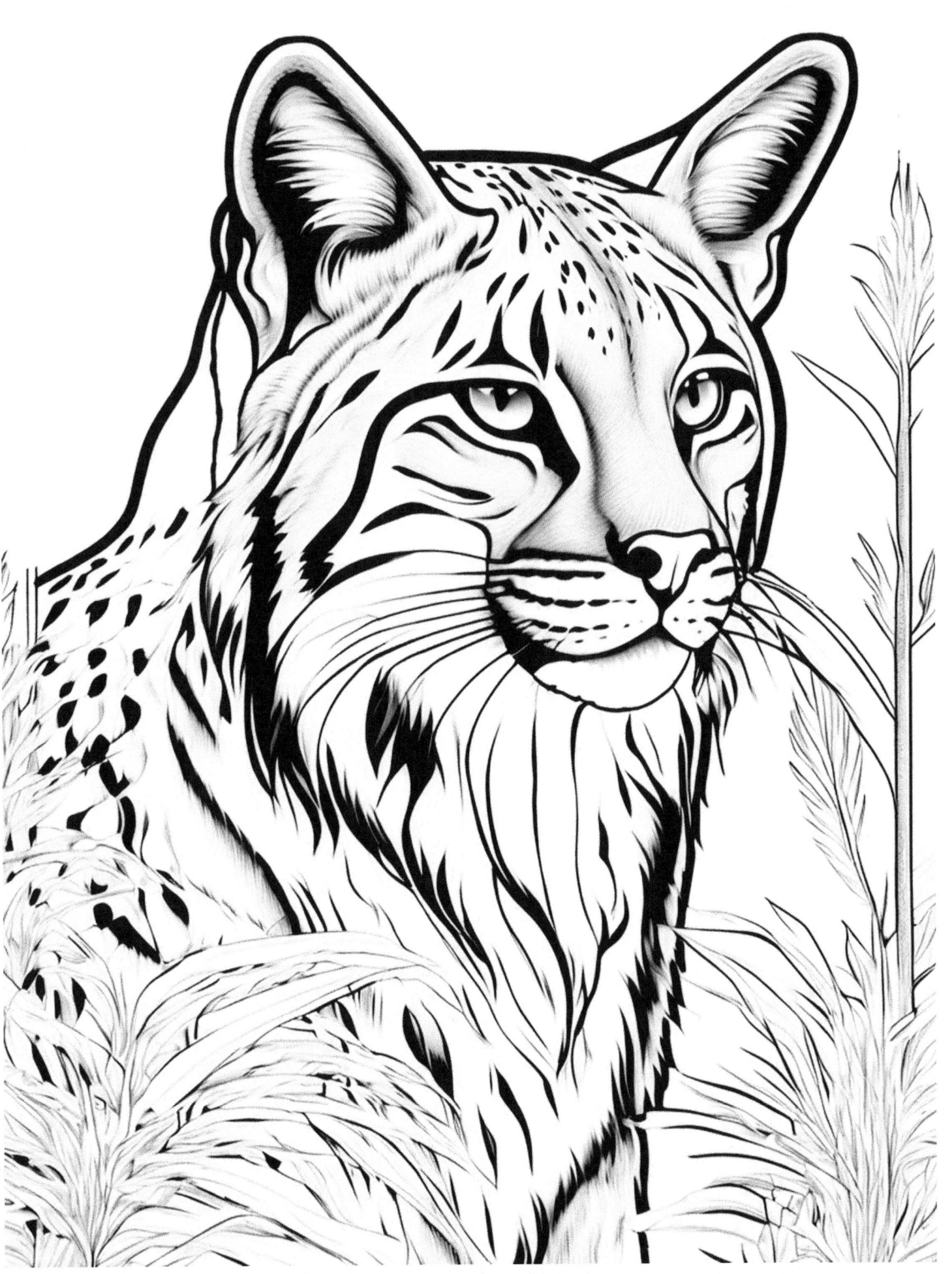

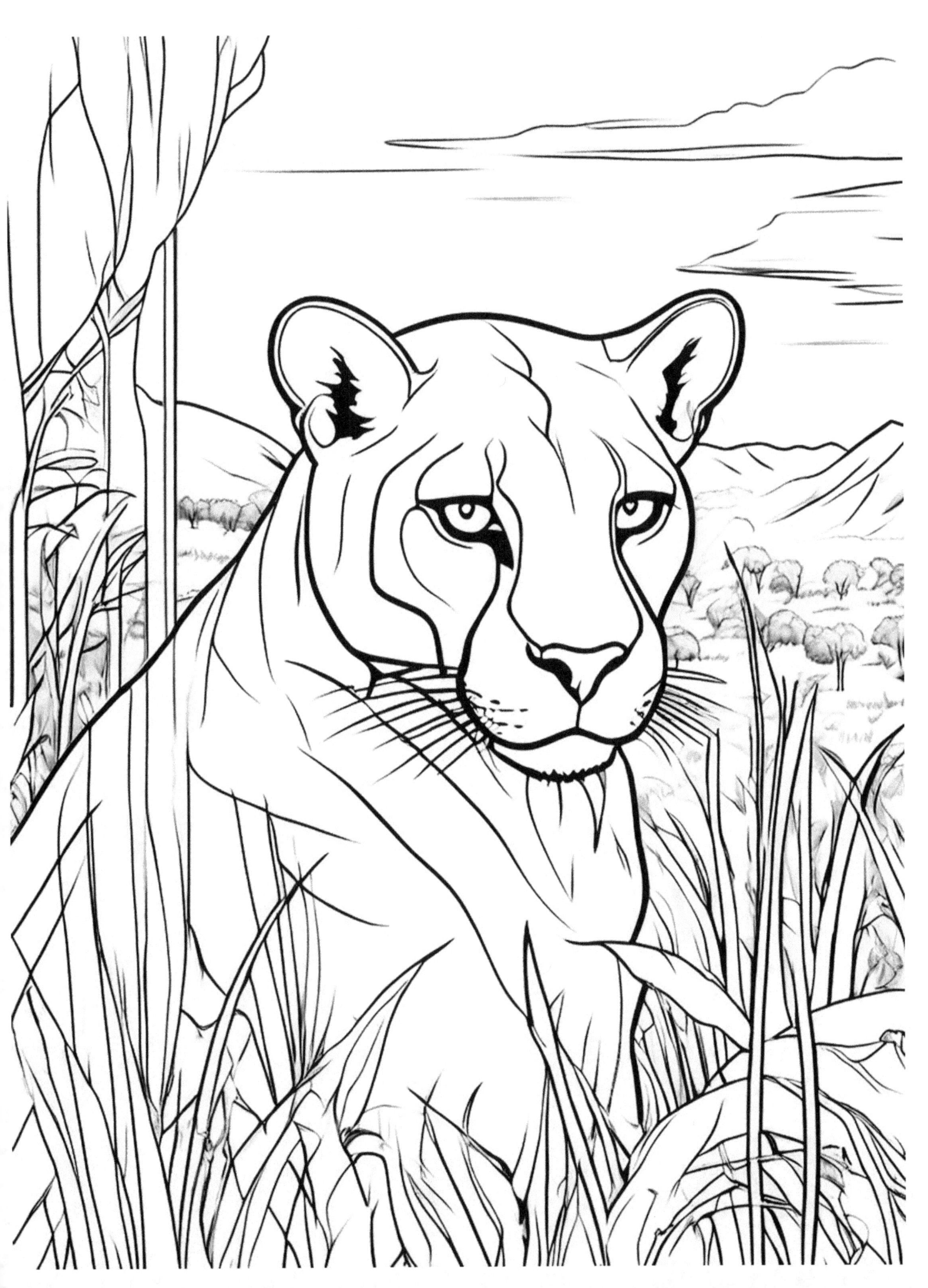

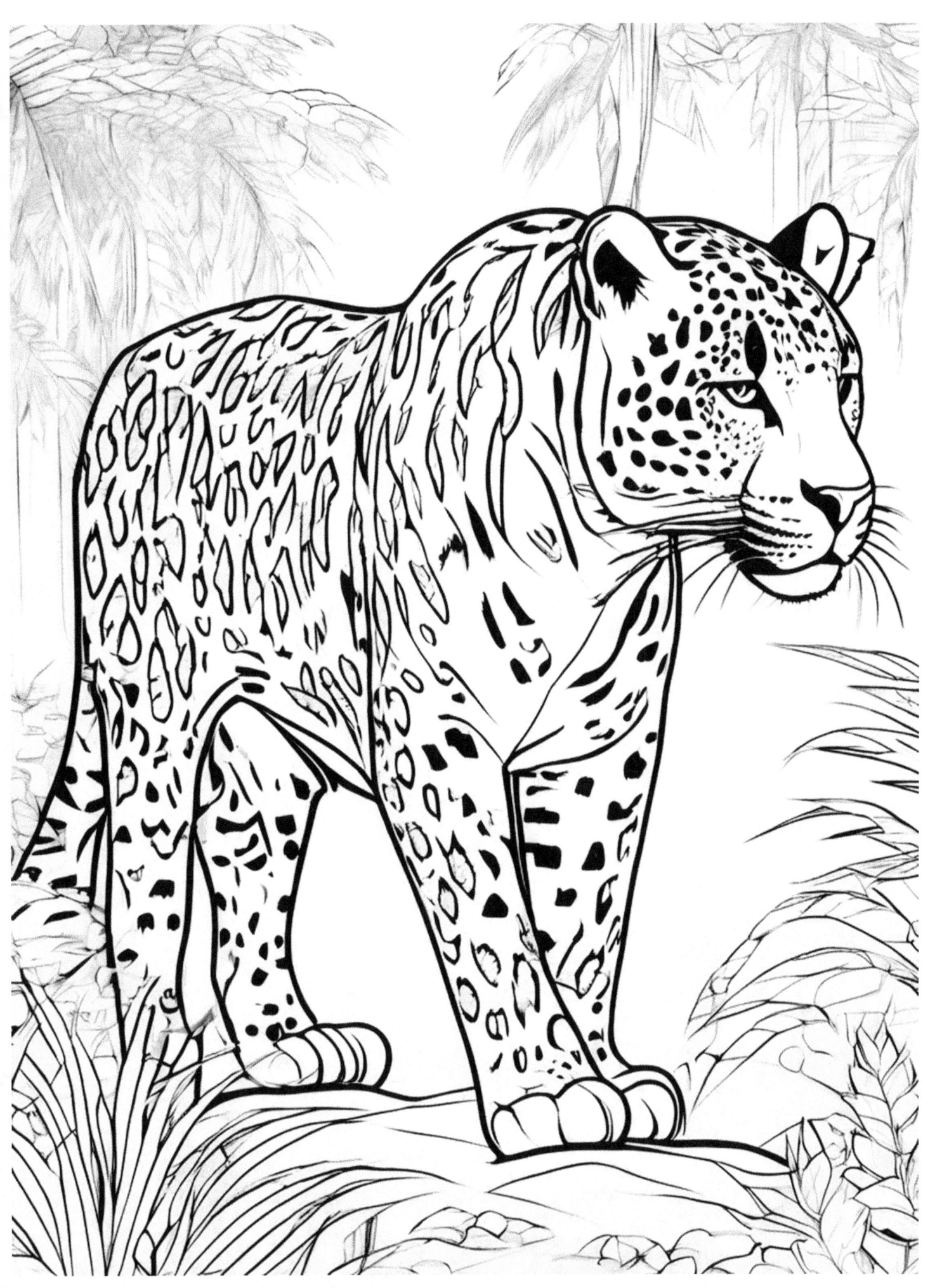

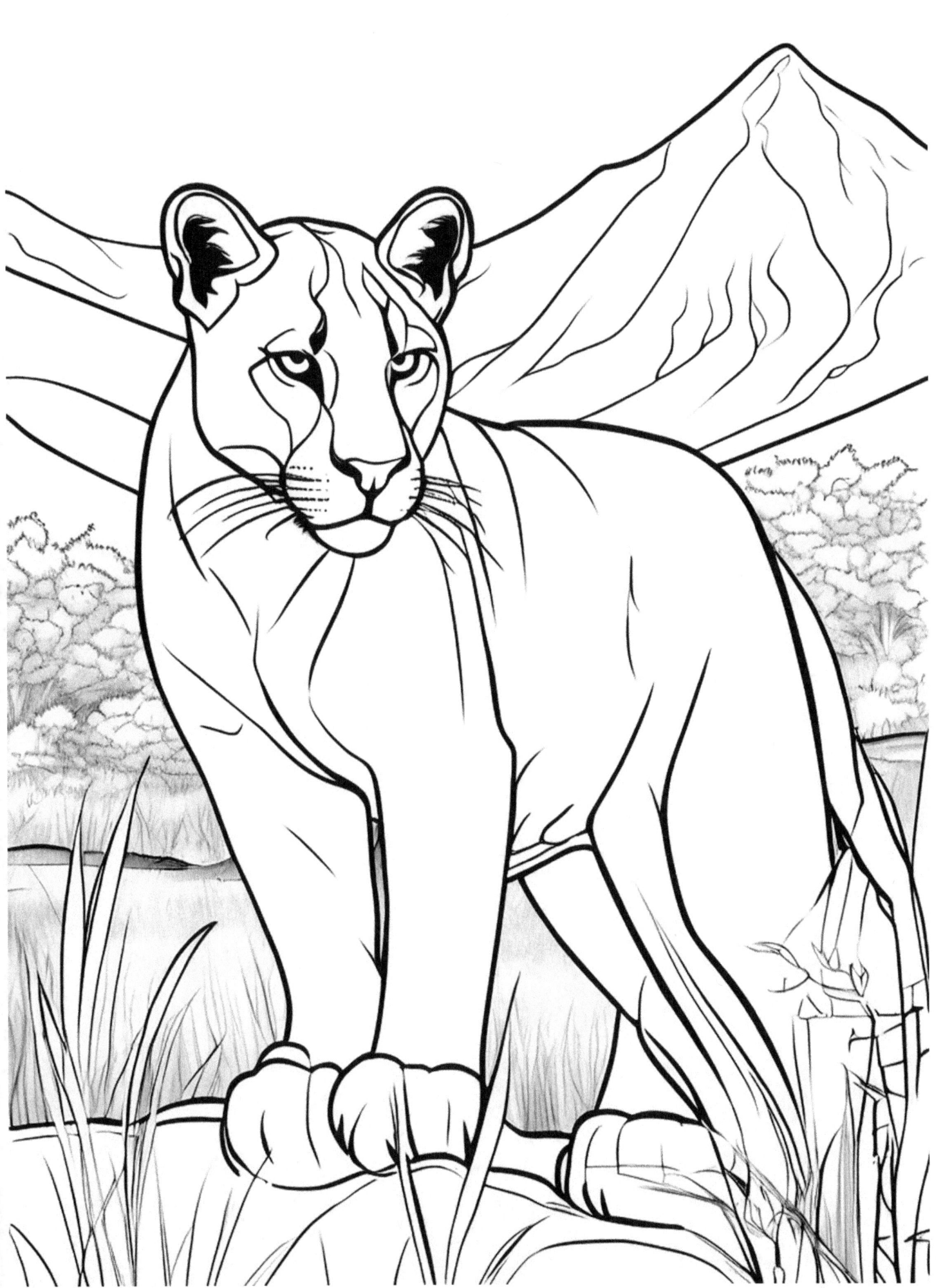

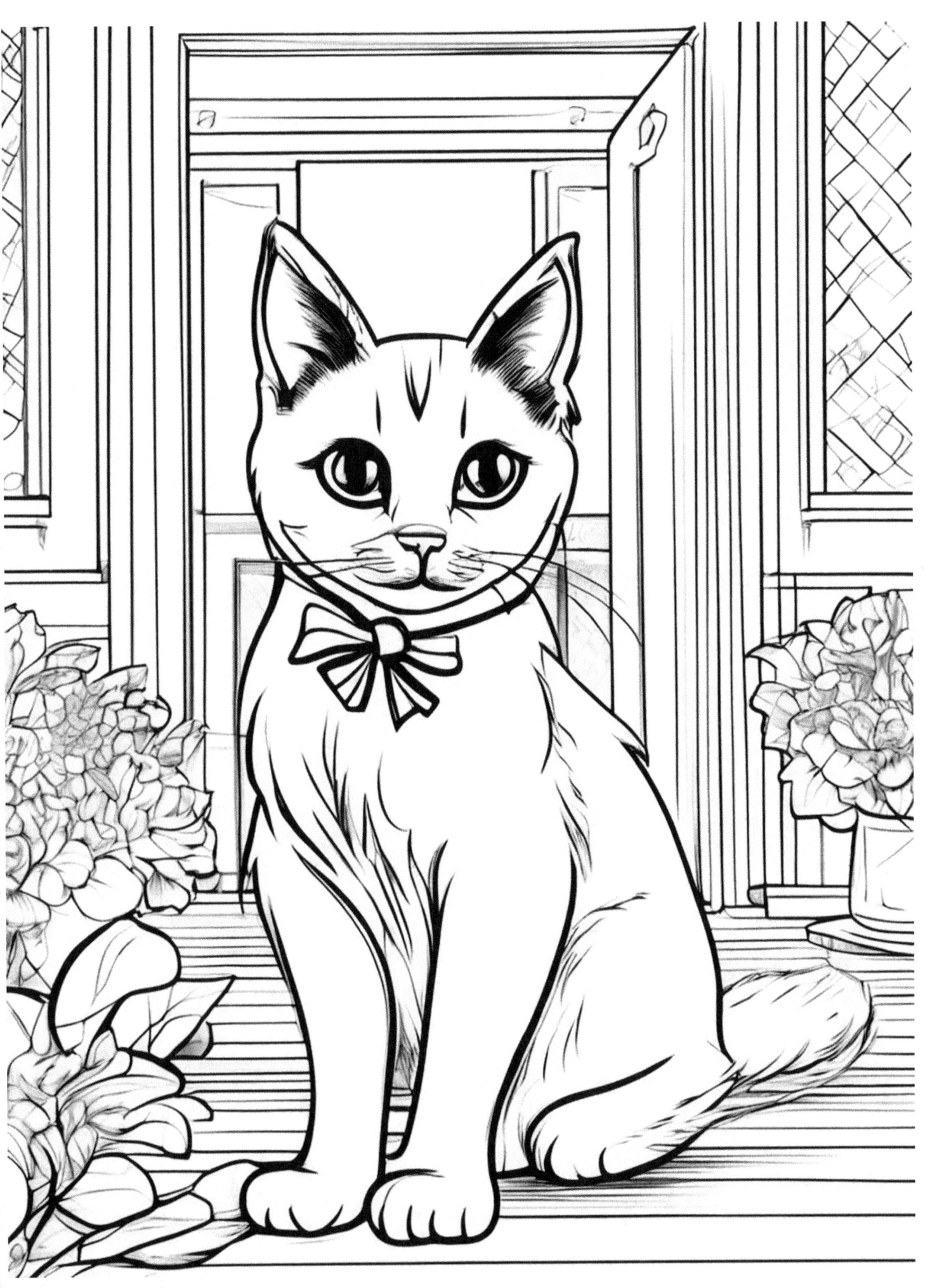

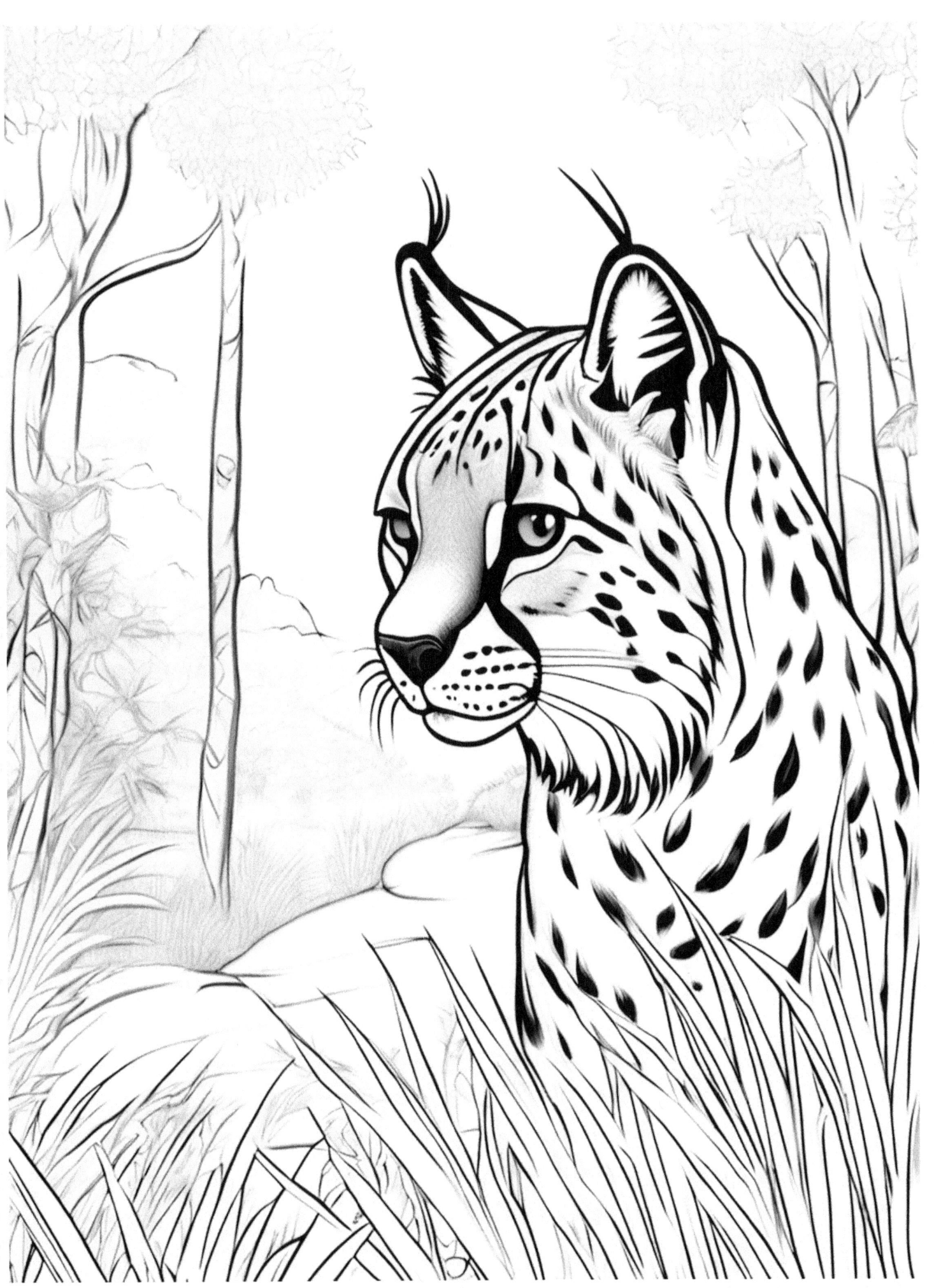

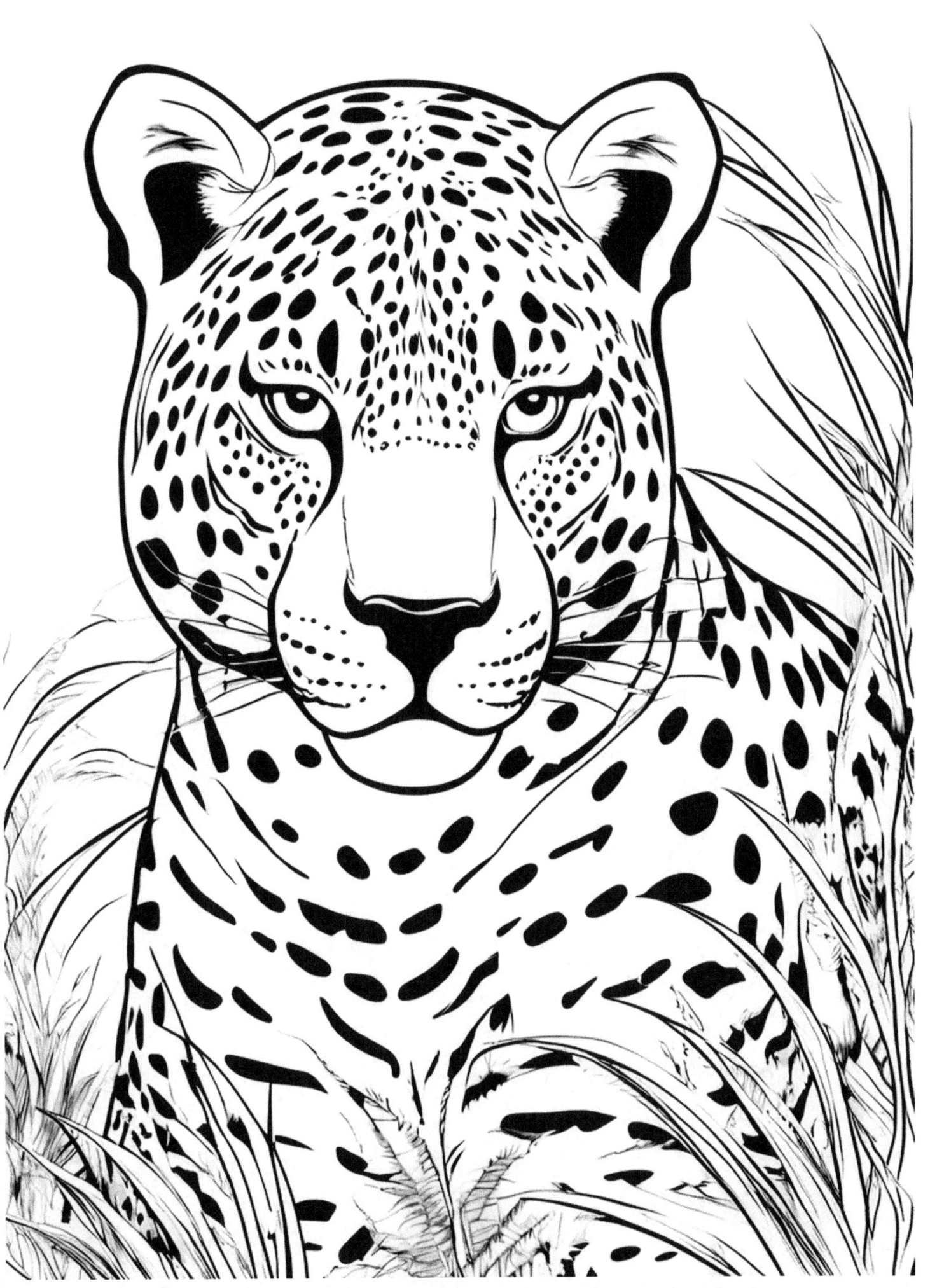

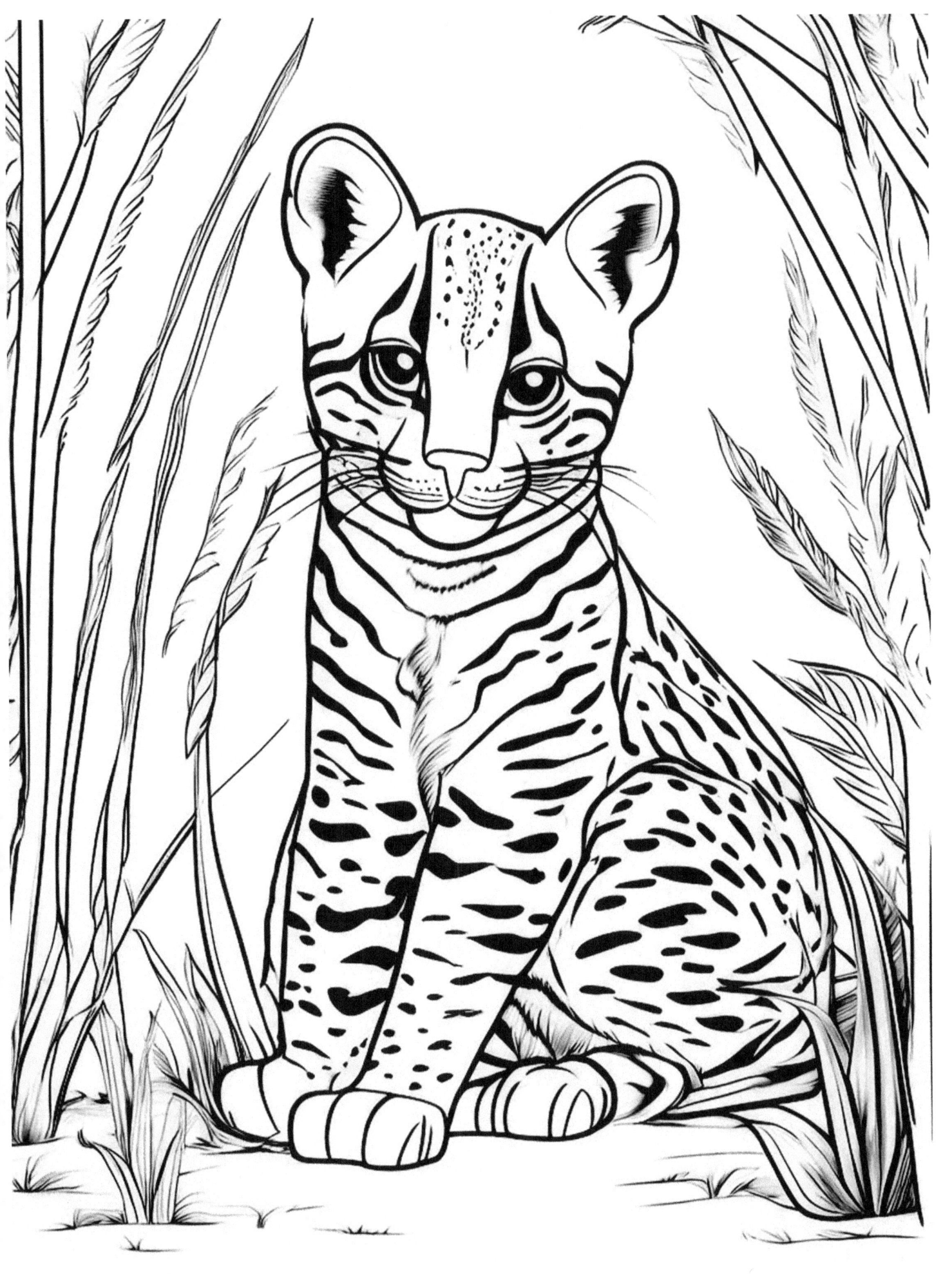

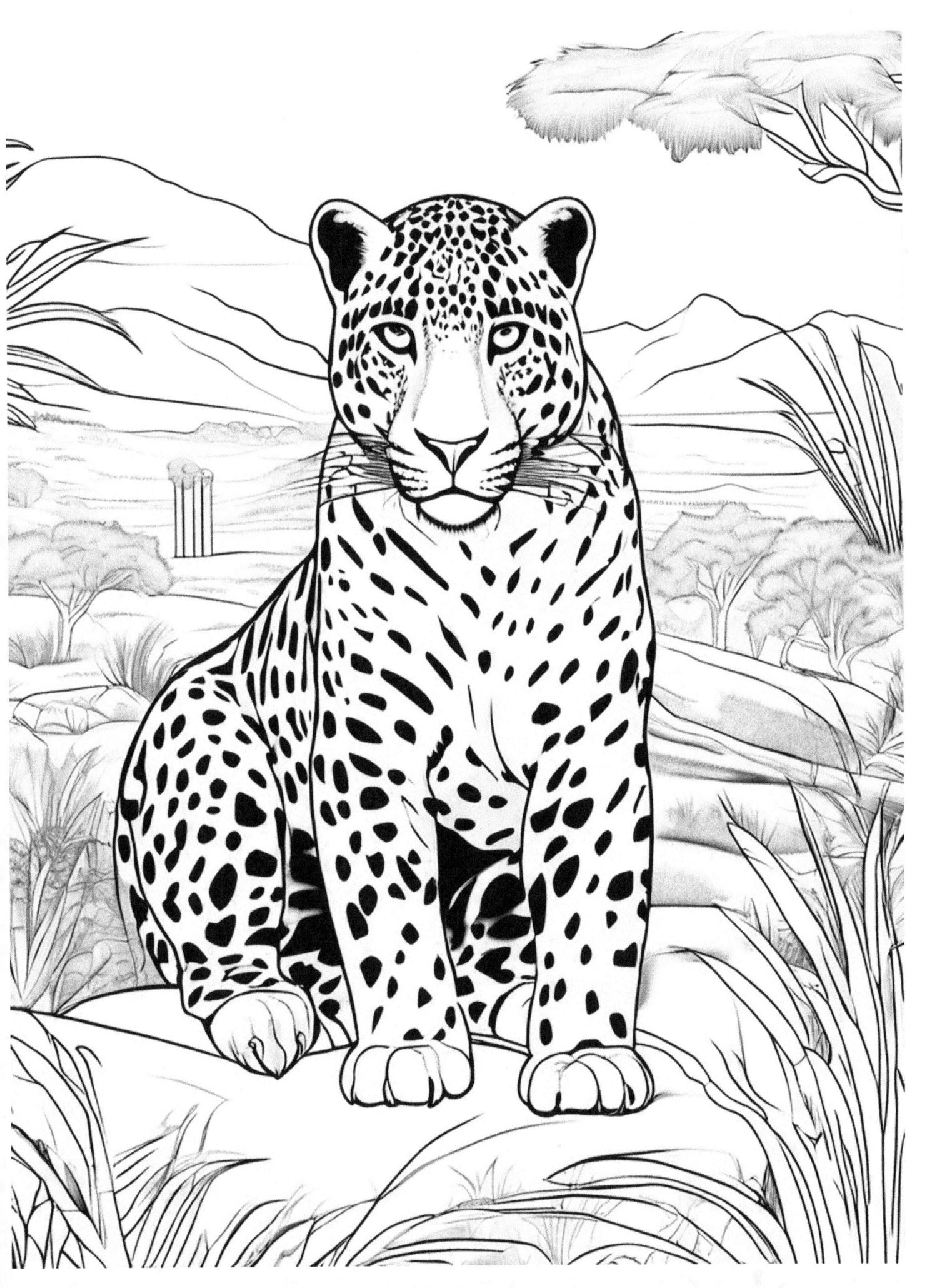

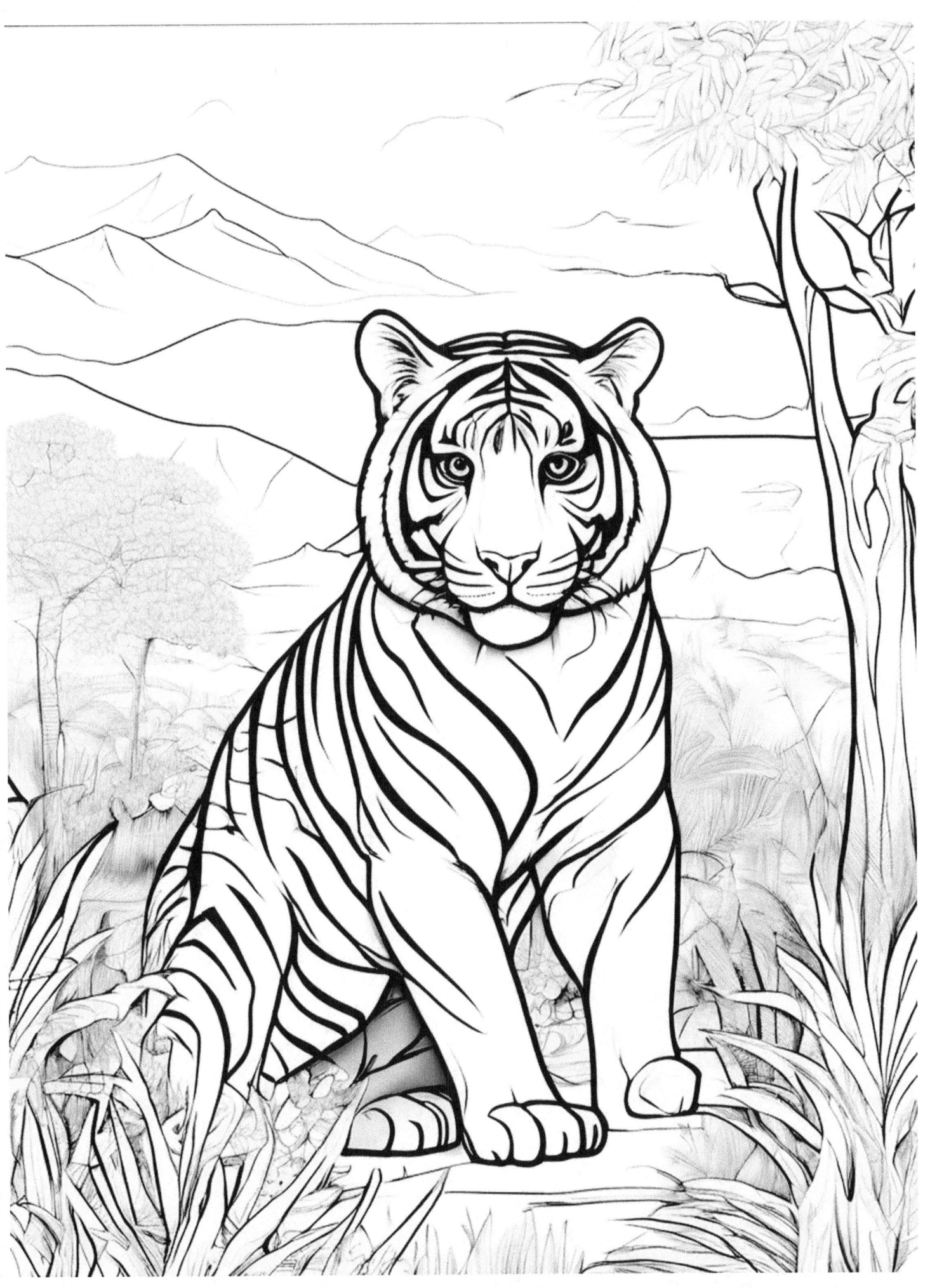

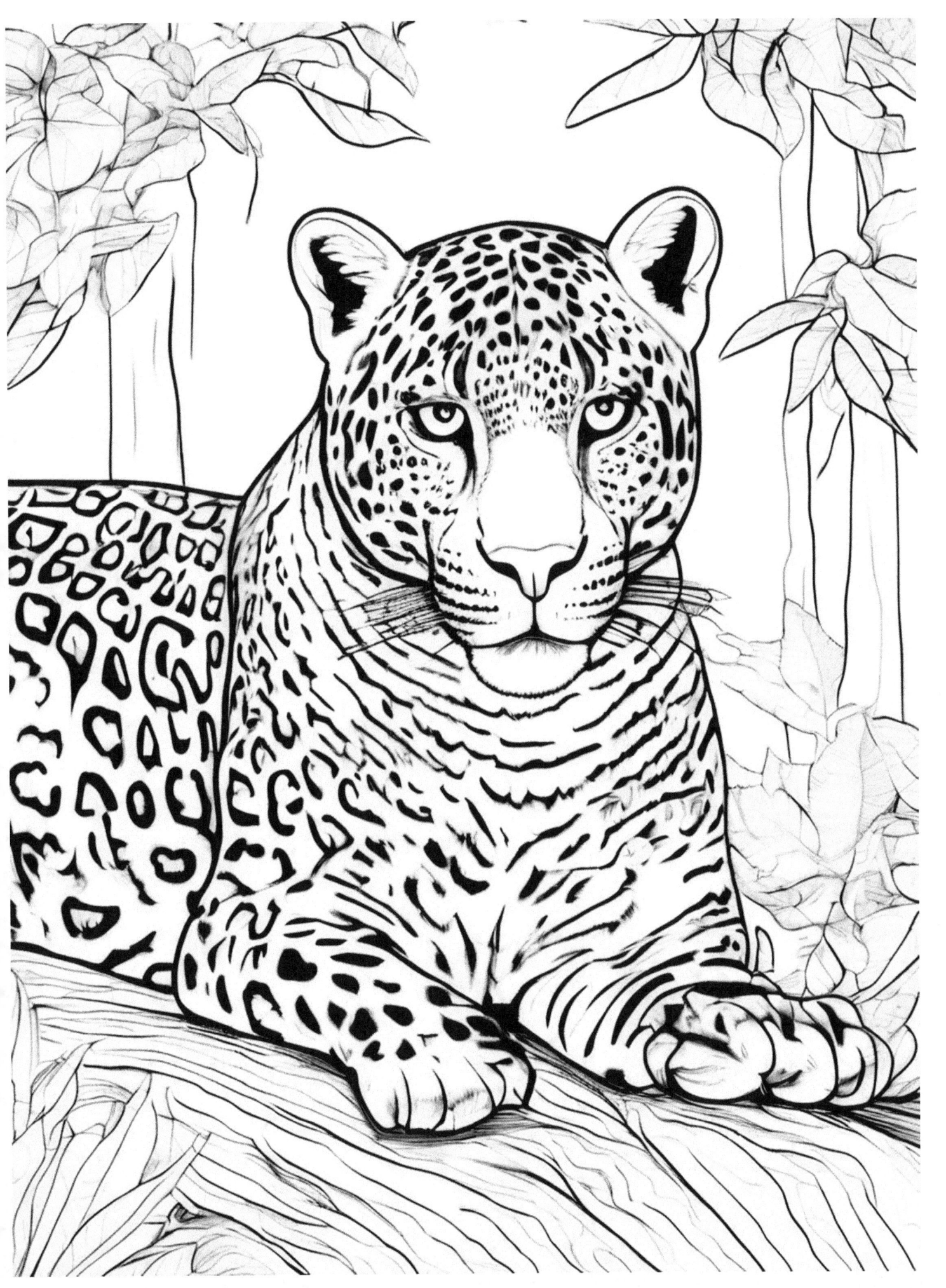

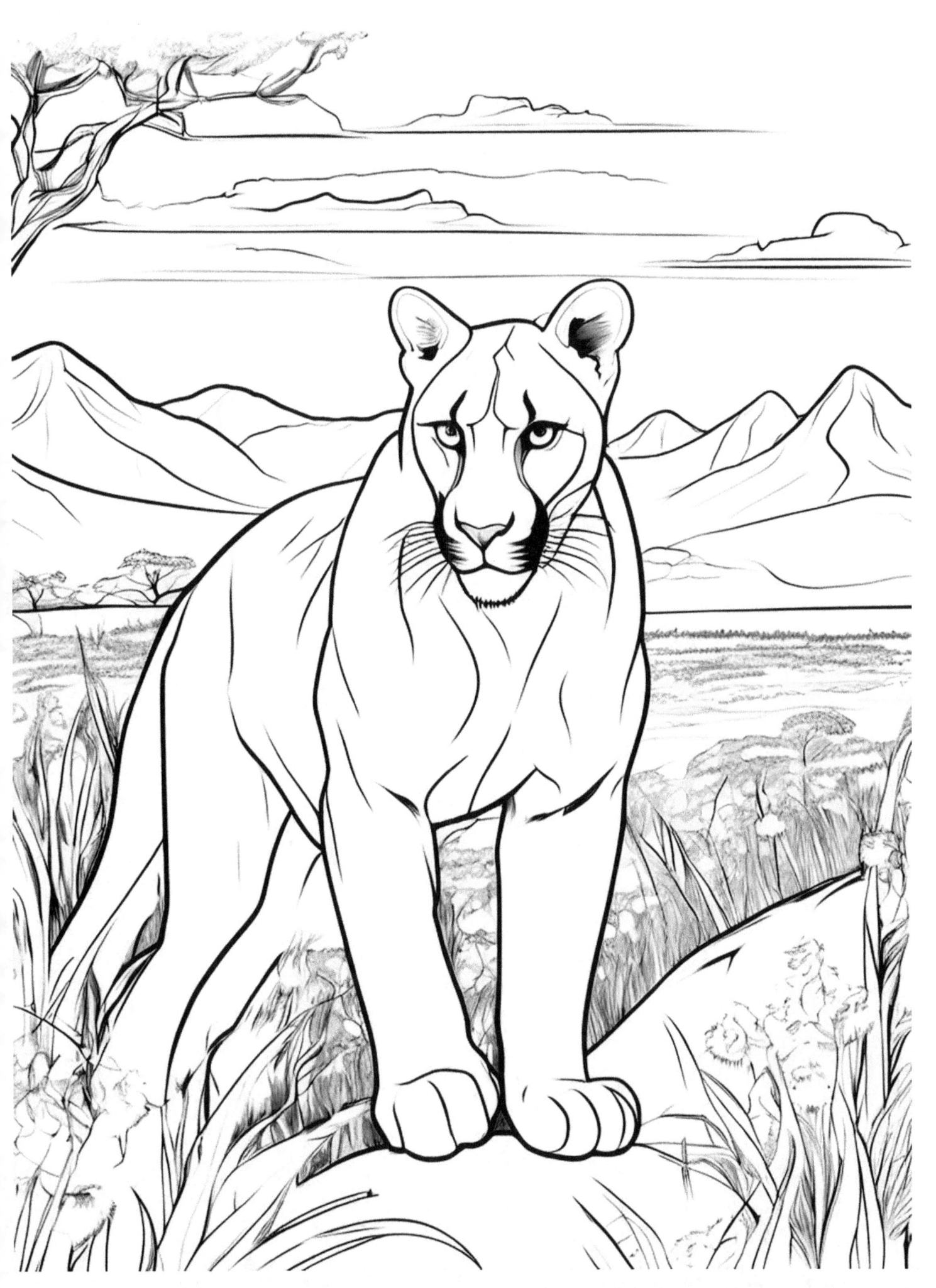

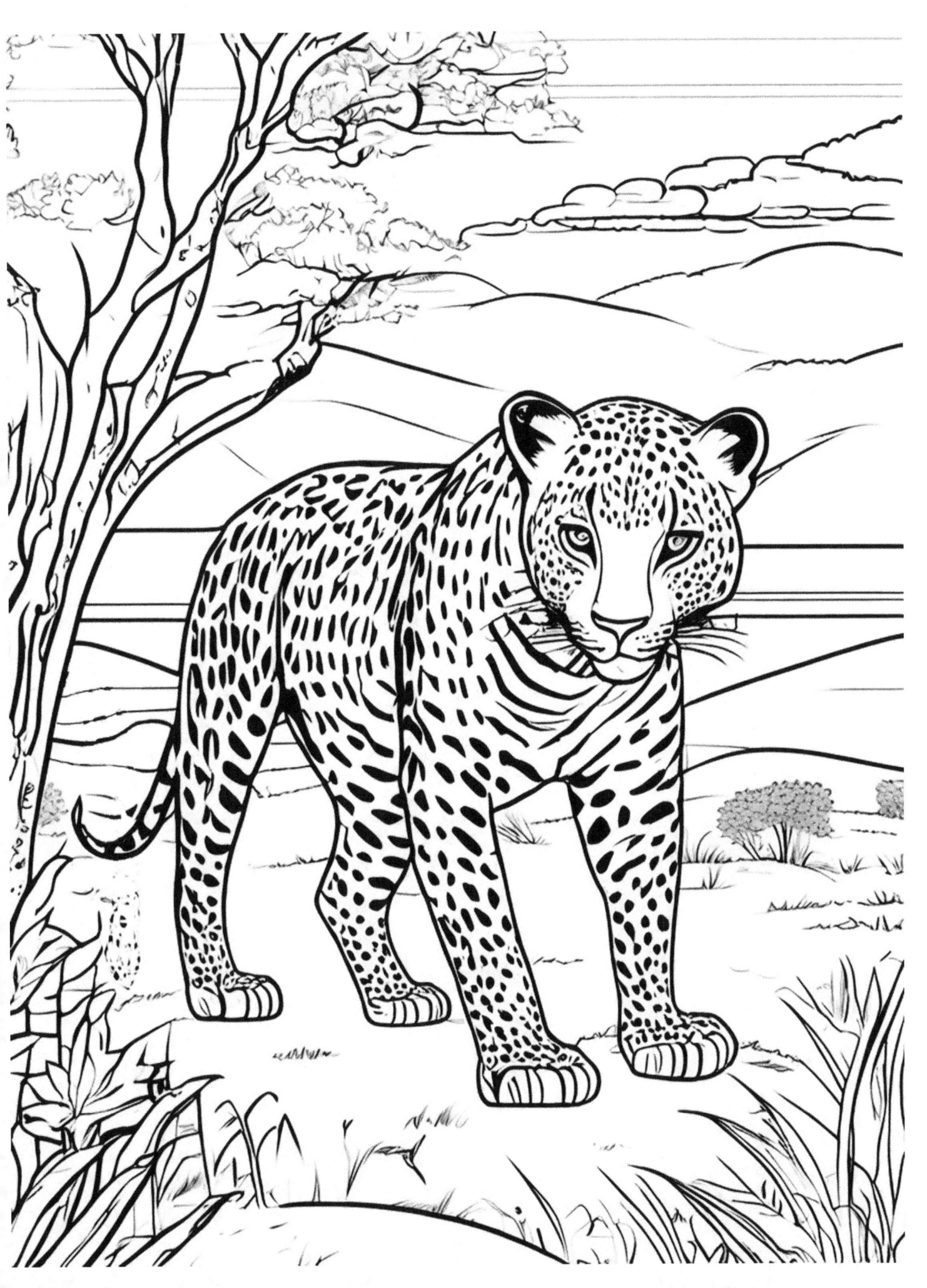

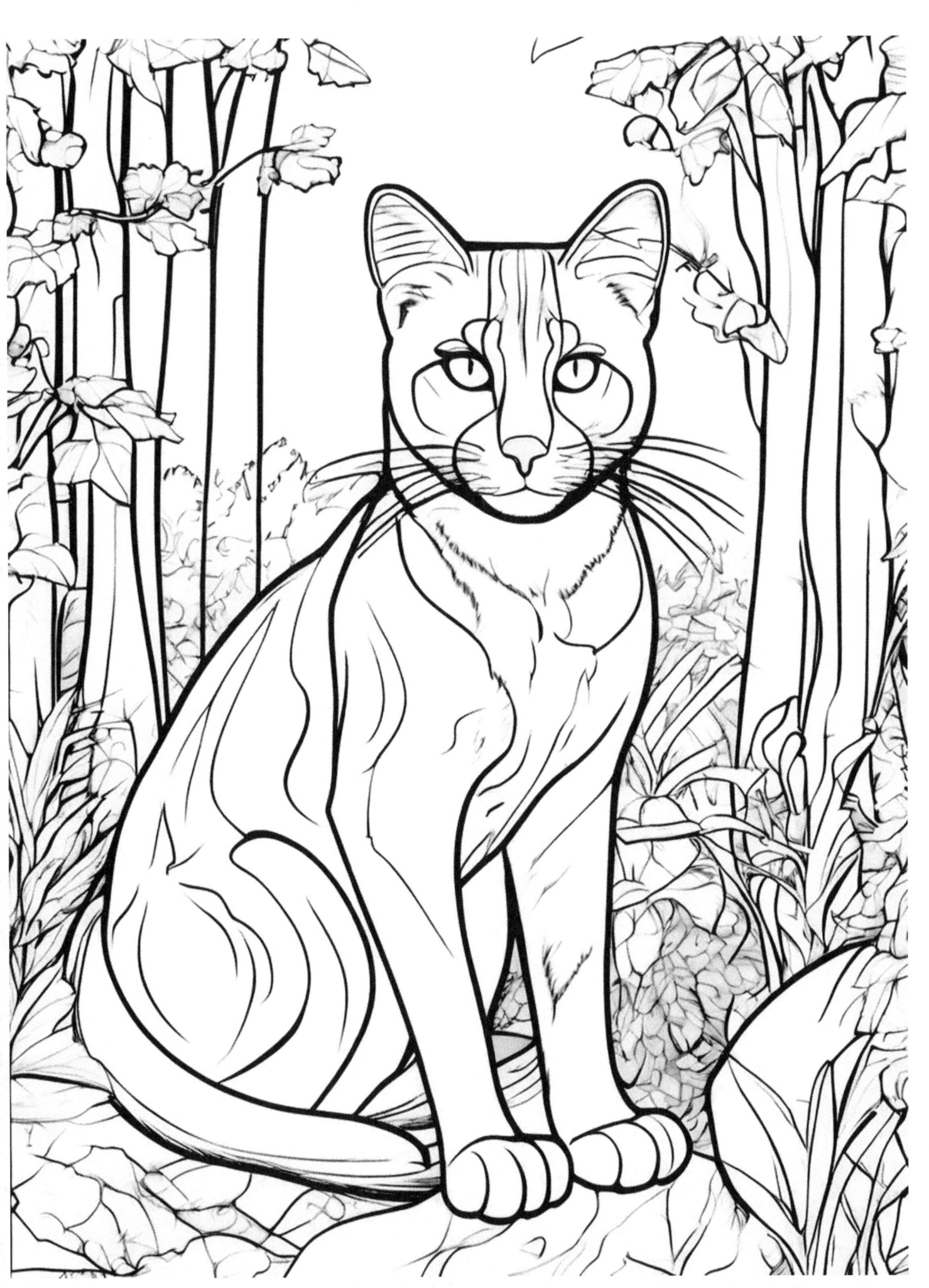

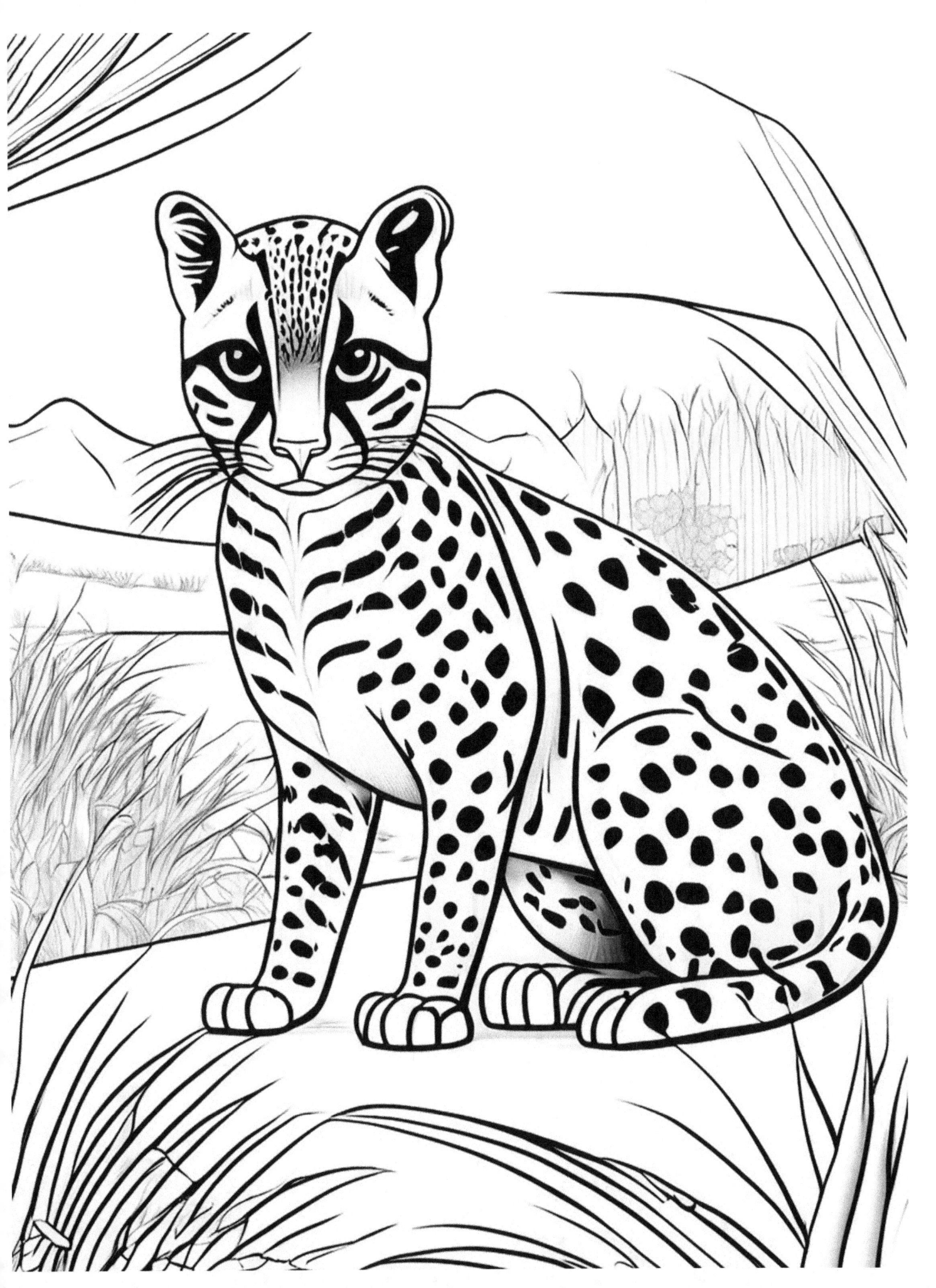

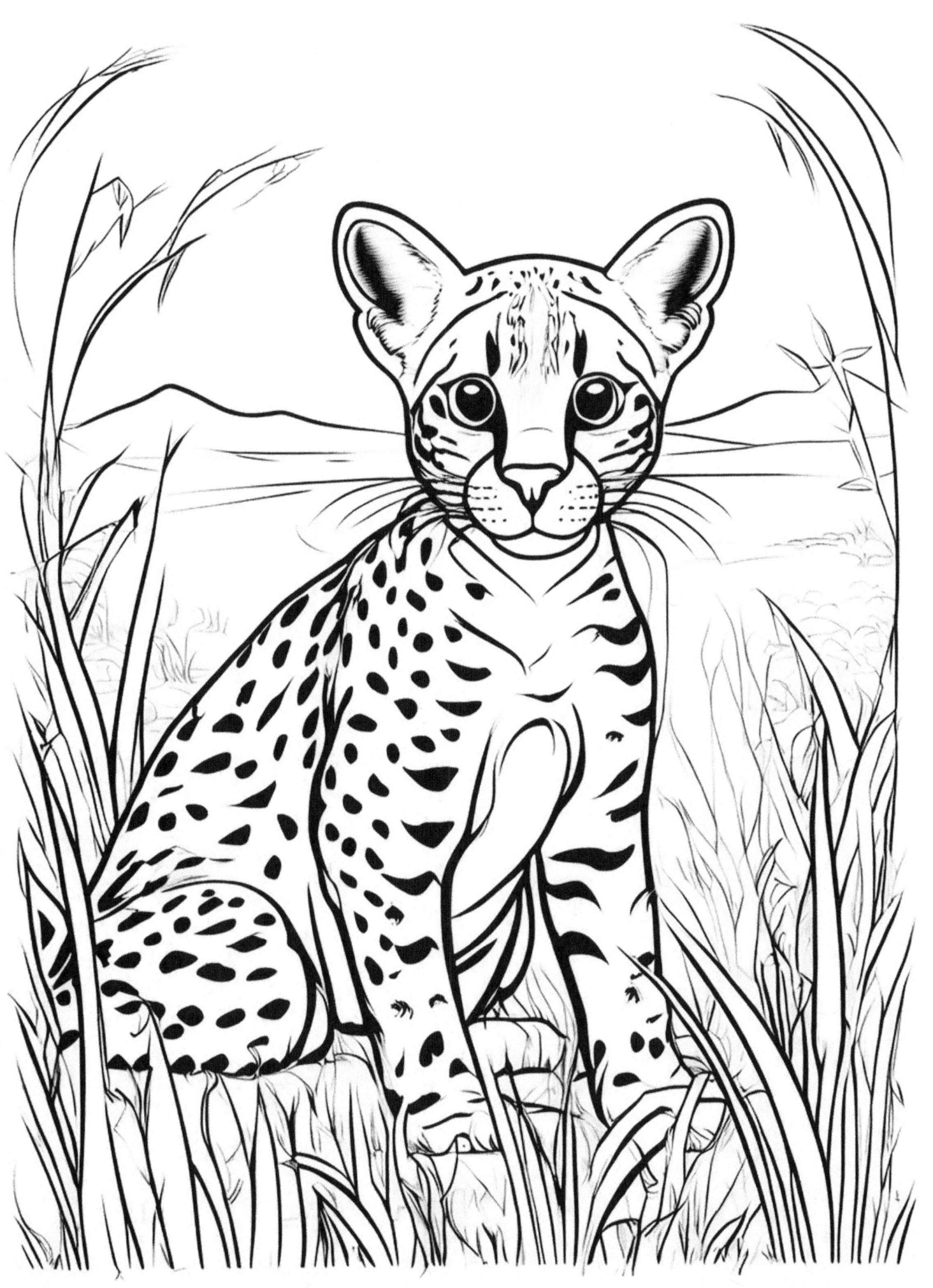

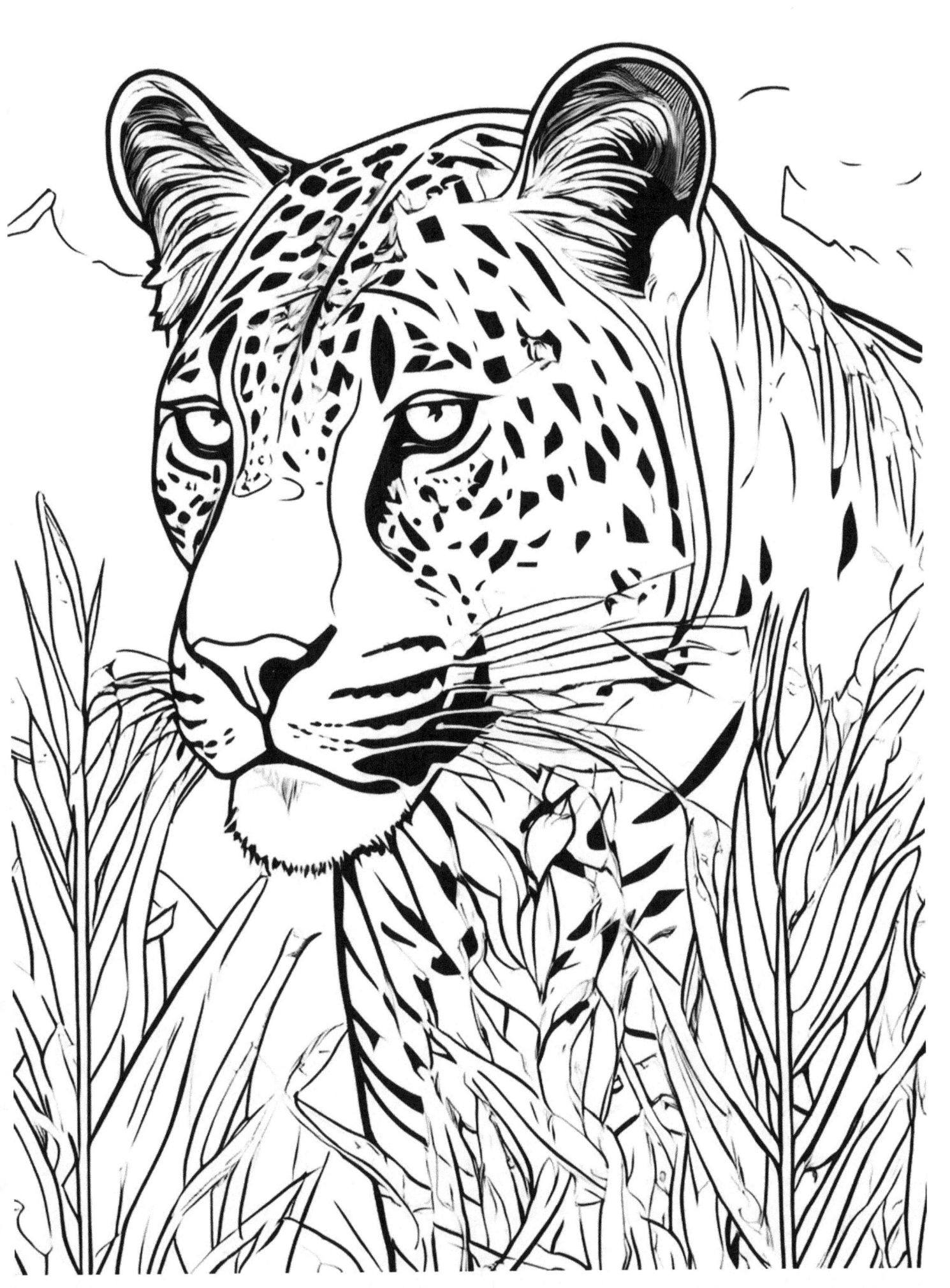

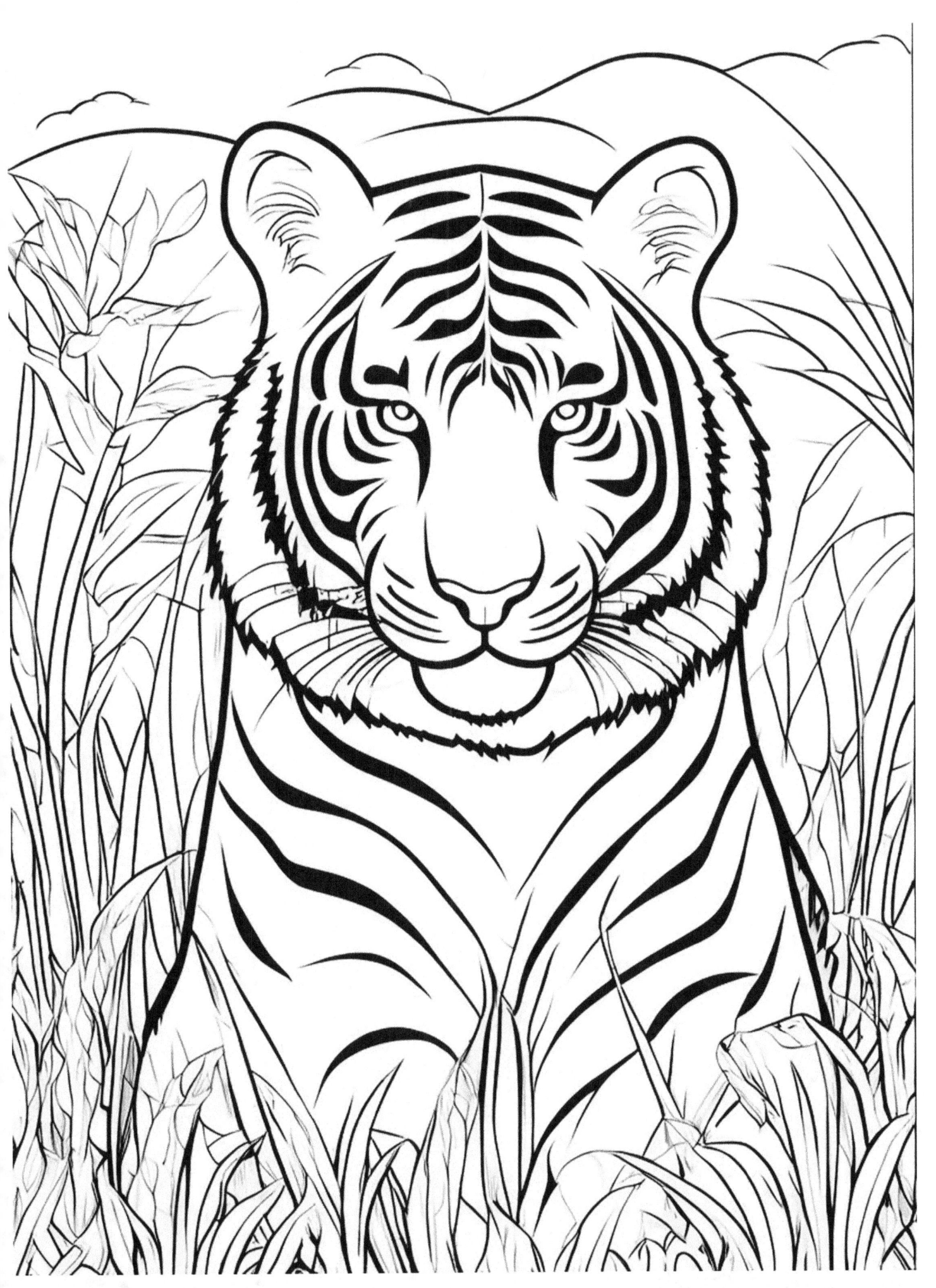

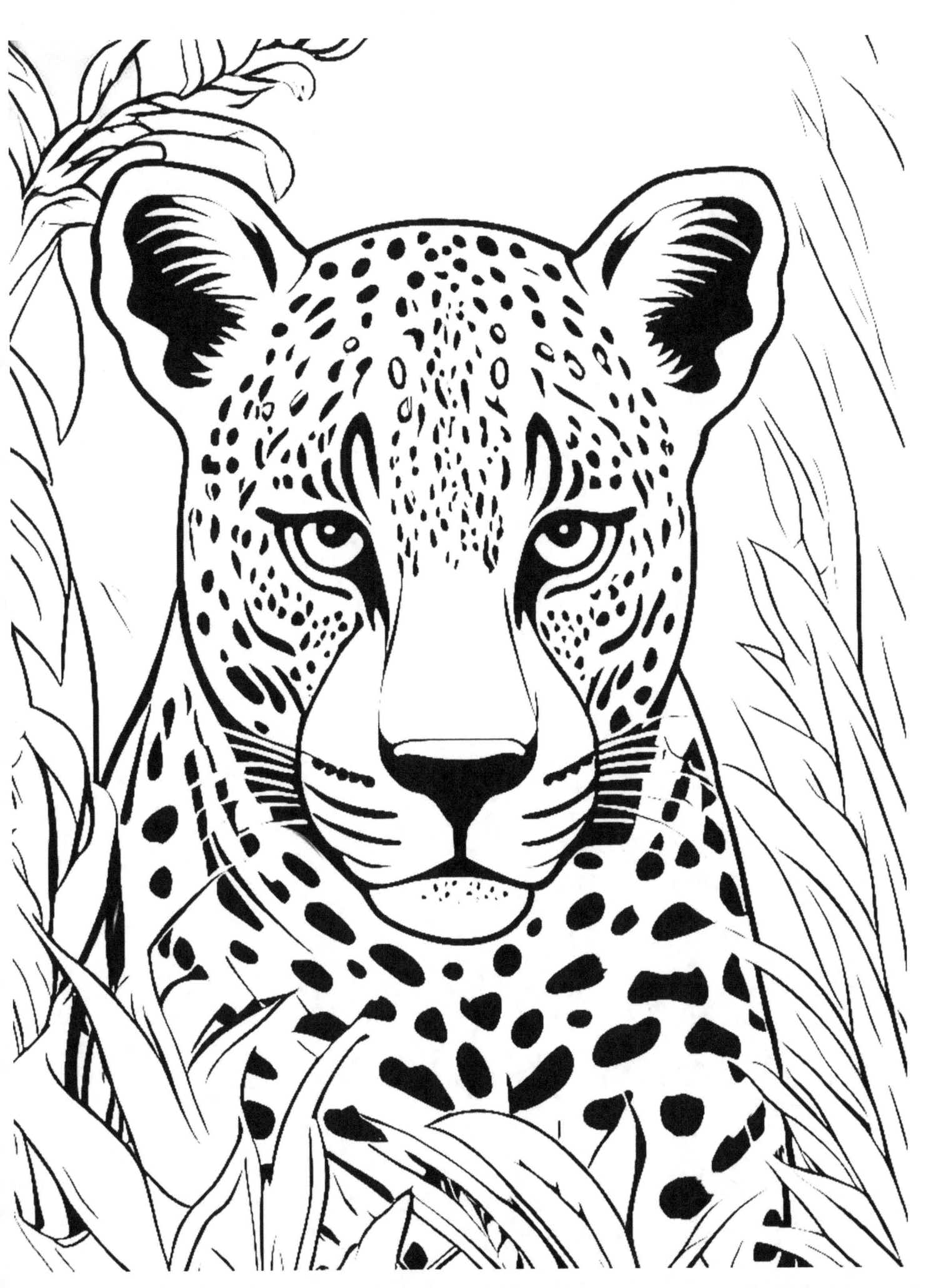

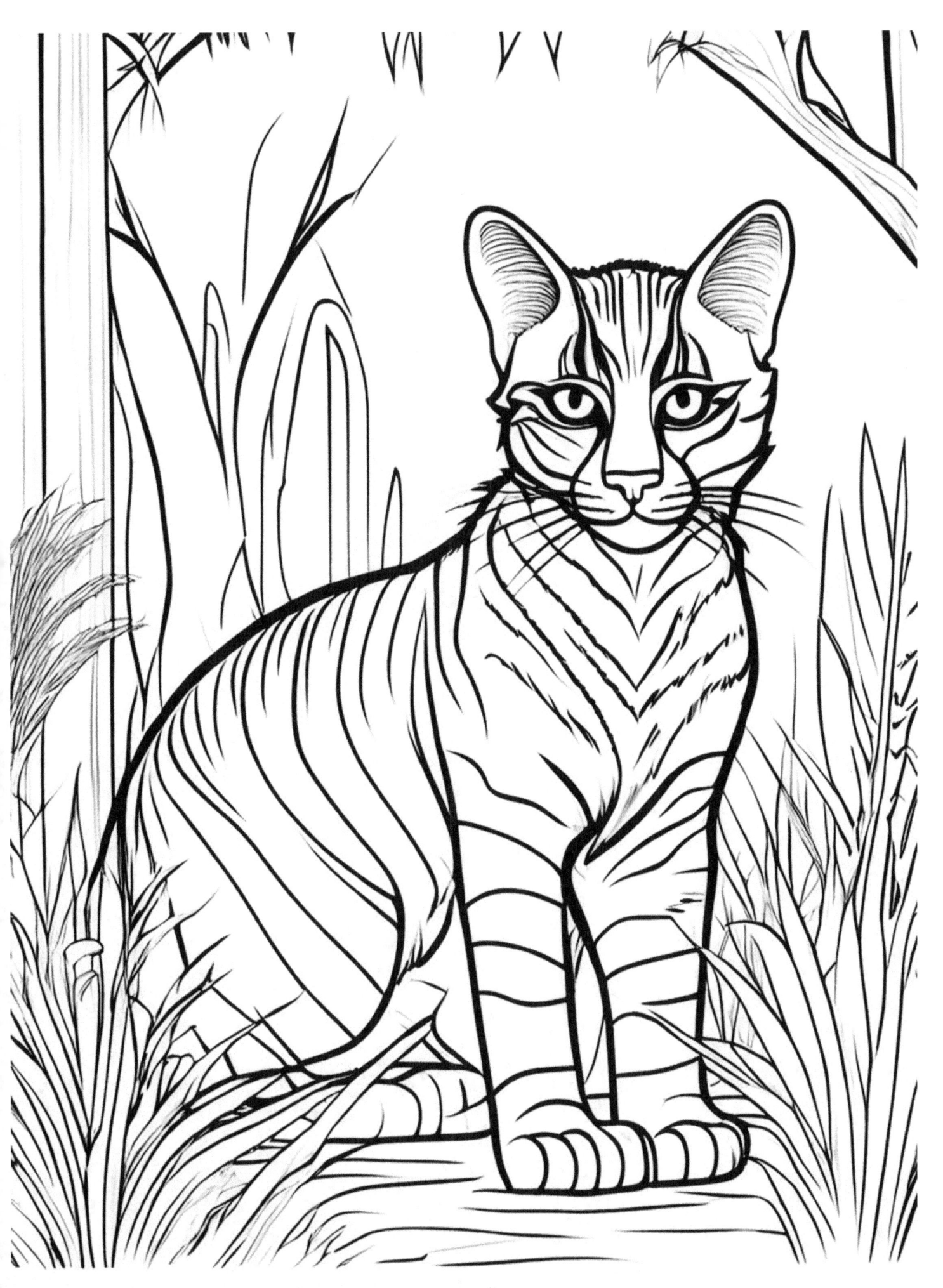

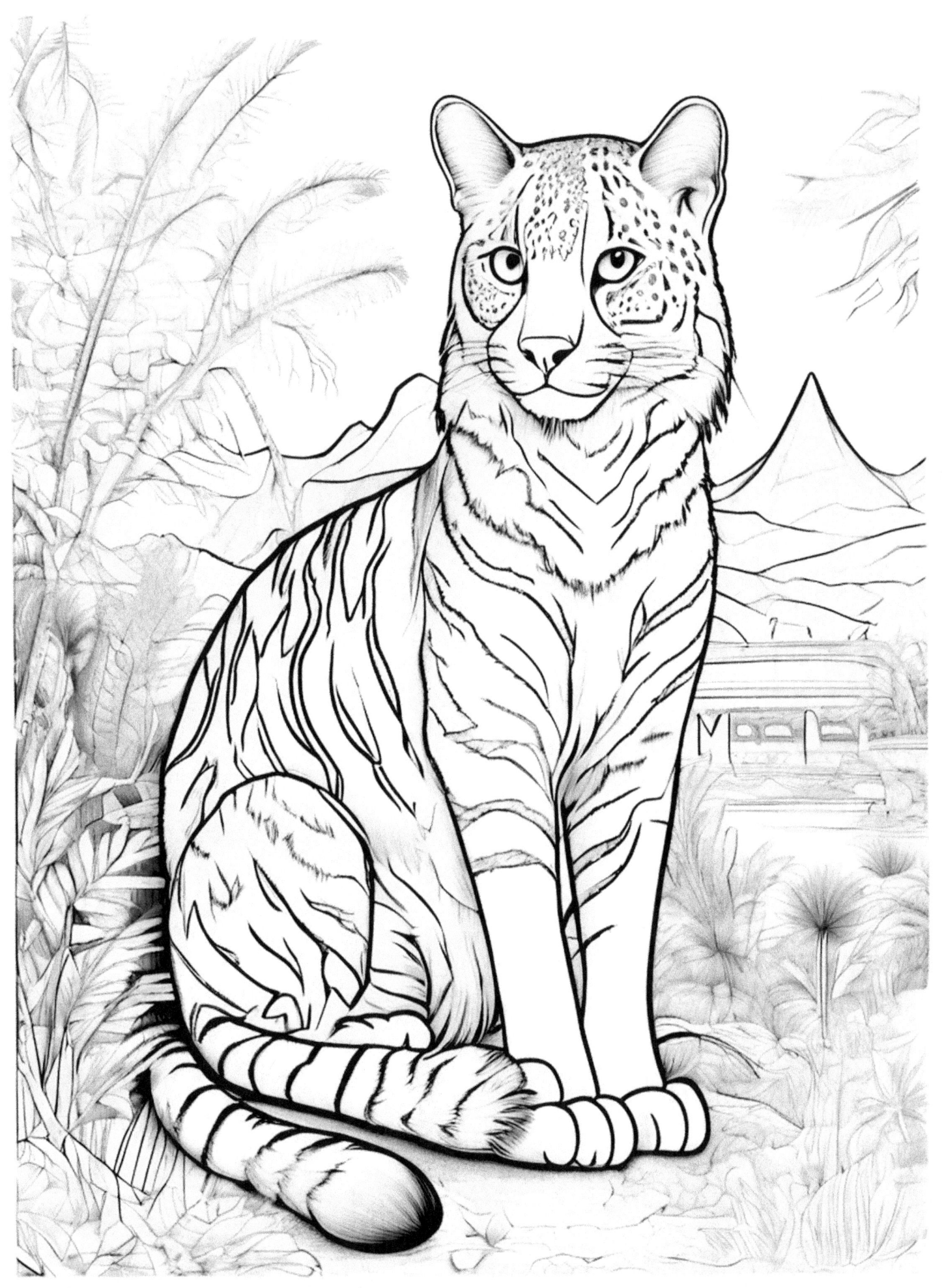

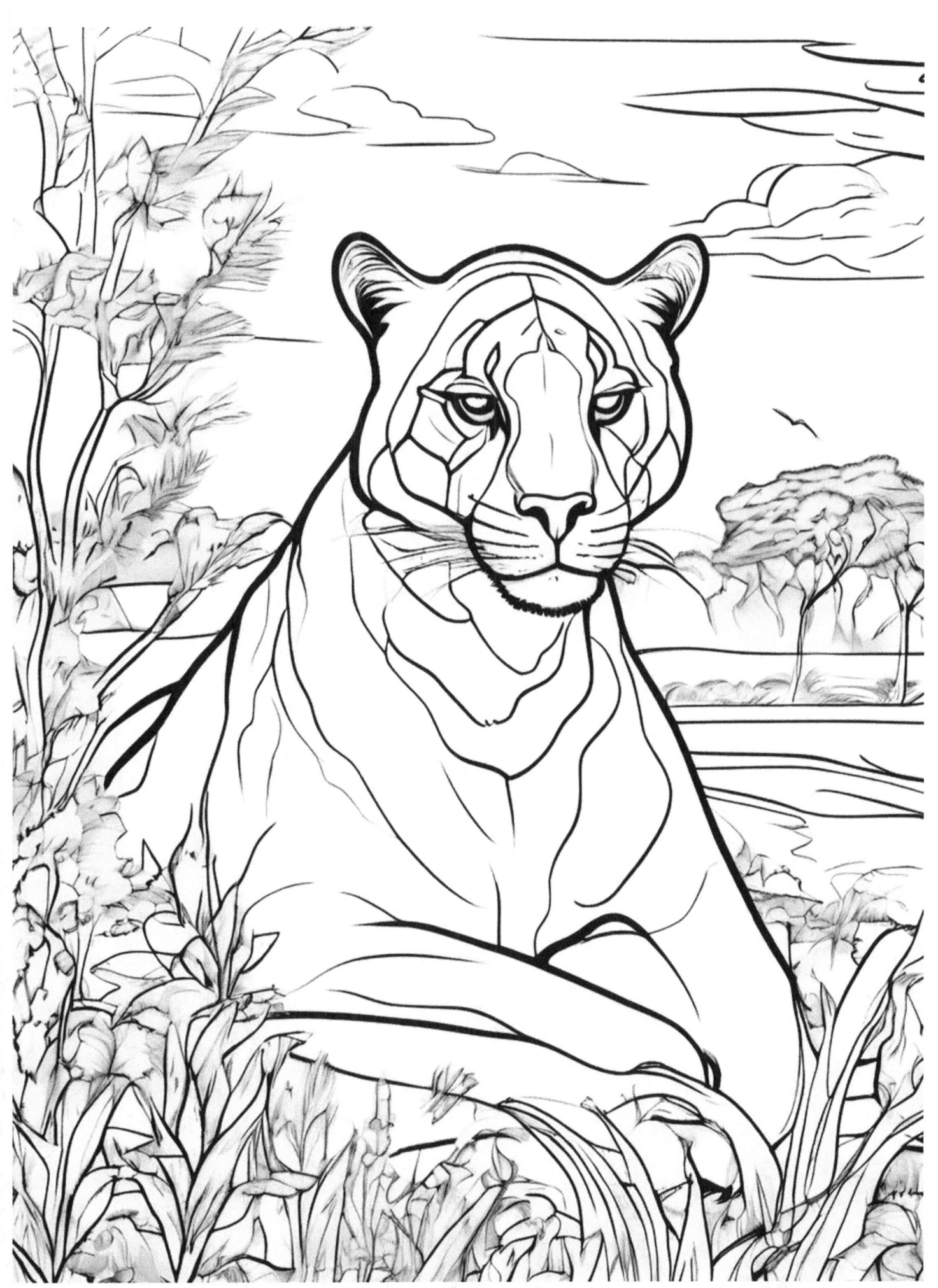

Thank you for purchasing our copy, enjoy it, we hope that this work will be of great benefit to you.

The End

www.ingramcontent.com/pod-product-compliance
Lightning Source LLC
Chambersburg PA
CBHW062122220526
45471CB00010B/3835